# Lessons

# Reworking Spiritual Paradigms

E S Carpenter

Copyright 2018 E S Carpenter

Disclaimer: Any enclosed description or resemblance to anyone living or deceased is unintentional and coincidental.

If negative emotional undertones are detected in this book; if the tone seems derogatory in any way, please note: it is not inferred by the author. For the written word, psychology has proven, emotional inflection is the creation of the reader and not necessarily* the writer. Please don't mis-associate or misconstrue a dissenting message with a derogatory tone. This message is written out of love. If I didn't care for you, I wouldn't jeopardize my health or waste my time writing this. I already know the enclosed information.

* unless the words are specifically/inarguably/personally insulting.

All work bracket enclosed [ ] is from the referenced source shared – and the work of the referenced site or author. Even the previous work of this author is [bracketed]. This book contains referenced and sited material from other sources. It is all [bracketed] and credited at the insert or in the end bibliography.

Note: The book's title refers to the lessons I've received. I write them with the hope, some will help you understand a greater reality.

TABLE of CONTENTS

Prologue

Chapter 1   Introduction Background & Message – 1

Chapter 2   God Paradigms – 11

    Love – 20

    Forgive – 28

    Love/Forgive – 35

Chapter 3   Perfect – 39

    Demands for Worship – 57

    Religion's Imperfect Explanation of Perfect – 61

Chapter 4   Love vs Hate – 65

Chapter 5   The Bible (In General) – 81

    Origins of the Bible – 85

    Moses – 91

    God vs The Bible – 96

Chapter 6   Reframing Bible Stories – 107

    Adam & Eve – 108

    Original Sin / Creation / Noah – 112

    The Dogmatic Description of God – 120

    Christ vs God the Creator – 123

Chapter 7   Earning Heaven – 129

    Bible Interpretation – 143

    Rewritings and Reinterpretations – 155

Chapter 8   Law vs Love – 179

    Law – 179

    Love – 181

Chapter 9   If God is Perfect… – 187

    Reincarnation – 187

    The Meaning of Life – 201

Chapter 10   Bible Specifics – 207

    The Ten Commandments – 209

    The tenth commandment – 218

    The Ark of the Covenant – 223

    How Many Commandments? – 224

Chapter 11   The Eradication of Hell – 227

    Bible Summation – 236

    The Sadducees vs Current Religions – 237

    Our Programming – 246

Chapter 12   LGBT Normality – 251

    Biblical Argument: LGBT Normality – 255

    Intellectual Argument: LGBT Normality – 274

Chapter 13   Legacy of Religion – 285

    The Earth's Dilemma – 288

    Tolerance and Acceptance – 289

    Coexist – 290

    Belittling Religion – 303

    The Multiple Generation Curse – 306

       To Muslim Brothers and Sisters – 307

       To the Next Generation – 308

       To my (our) 'Imperfect Children' – 314

       To Brothers and Sisters – 315

       To Educators – 317

       To Government Leaders – 318

Chapter 14   Change – 323

       The Future – 324

       Conclusion – 326

       Our Free Will – 332

       Personal Conclusion – 338

Addendum – 341

Bibliography – 345

Post Script – 349

**PROLOGUE:**

The problem isn't what we don't know. It's what we think we know that isn't actually so. – Will Rogers

We learn something every day, and lots of times, it's that what we learned the day before ... was wrong. – Bill Vaughan

I believe the enclosed information and have gathered enough verification to share it with a clear conscience. I cannot measure whether or not it's exact truth, but believe the information accuracy would rank high in syllogistic logic and criterion analysis. I don't have access to the cosmic rubric, but believe the information is closer to the truth than some two-thousand-year-old perspectives currently believed unquestioningly.

# Chapter One
## Introduction & Message

If you are not part of the solution, you are part of the problem. – Eldridge Cleaver (a variation of the original quote)

Hell's warmest places are reserved for those who remain indifferent in times of moral strife. – Dante Alighieri (a variation of the original quote)

Here we are. Witnessing another dividing point in human history. But don't think it's monumentally significant or rare. They're not. Opportunities to adjust our course of existence, appear frequently. But here we are nonetheless, with another chance to make decisions that will affect the future. And it's our choice whether or not we act on the moment before it passes again and we get further entrenched in our current direction.

The unrecognized problem: When these opportunities arise, the average person is unprepared to fully evaluate the circumstance and unable to make completely informed decisions on a new course of action.

If you interpreted that statement to mean, most people lack a certain level of intelligence, you've misunderstood the message. The sentence actually refers to the self-declared significance of the pertinent information, more than the intelligence of the human.

Educational psychology proves, almost all people have the same intelligence. We can all store – four plus or minus two bits of information in our current memory. Some people choose to manipulate certain bits of information enough to move them to short-term, then long-term memory. Others don't find particular bits of information interesting or worthy enough to do so. But, with rare exception, we all have the same intelligence, and Educational Psychology has proven this repeatedly.

The reasons why levels of insignificance are adopted, are more concerning. We're uncomfortable with change. Change creates great uncertainty and trepidation. Voluntarily adapting to the uncertainty of change opposes everything our being desires, but our current level of status quo is proving detrimental to our existence. Resisting change is human, but evolution demands adaptation, in order to survive.

The book will dissect the assumptions associated with our existing spiritual and cultural status quo and bring an awareness to current cultural beliefs which are not congruent with their foundational axioms. Other discussions will address the foundational source of some long-standing beliefs. And this new awareness may persuade you to further verify or refute spiritual paradigms which affect our societal existence.

Good judgment comes from experience, and experience comes from bad judgment. – Barry LePatner

This book analyzes foundational paradigms, which are so old and embedded in our culture, most individuals feel they no longer need or deserve questioning. Sadly, this assumption is based on one primary inaccuracy:

Ethnocentrism -  The idea those living two to three thousand years ago, had the same universal understanding and access to information, as our current human community.

And that inaccuracy is causing a rift between newly discovered truth and long believed lies.

This book addresses that difference, but you don't have to find the information significant enough to retain or use. As previously mentioned, opportunities come rather frequently. But the associated awareness might allow you take advantage of current societal opportunities.

Well-entrenched paradigms will be revisited, based on some unusual experiences and these experiential viewpoints will offer a unique look into our spiritual foundation. They also offer a new perspective on a Creator who deserves a more modern and current understanding and assessment.

Some enclosed perspectives might benefit those confused by the current interpretation of God. The current interpretation isn't positive or accurate, and some of the inaccuracies are having a negative effect on our human relationships and potential.

The perspectives enclosed are atypical, but the primary document used to validate the book's viewpoints is surprisingly well established. The homework has been done, and you'll be able to easily verify the principal references.

Other points will reference your cosmic being; allowing experiential logic to verify or refute the discussion points. Please consider doing so intellectually, and avoid judging this work based on hearsay, emotions, or unverified unsubstantiated cultural paradigms.

Please don't refute this perspective solely because you've been taught to, and if you're so inclined, please don't read this document. This document is intended for those able to reassess seemingly inarguable beliefs, and not meant for those wishing to continue living, without examining unproven archetypes.

Please measure the enclosed words without association to existing paradigms. Past beliefs should not influence or contradict our natural instinct, and when they do, it should trigger our awareness. But we've become so content in our ideologies, this incongruency seldom does. If these new perspectives show reason and sound argument, please consider analyzing them further and possibly adding them to your personal beliefs. They may help you decide future paths of action.

Also understand, the contents are controversial and will invoke great subjective scrutiny by those with far greater social standing, and alternate agendas hidden behind differing levels of self-servitude. That doesn't mean the longstanding dissention isn't flawed. It just means, a more objective intellectual discussion is necessary.

> What is to give light must endure burning. – Victor Frankl

The principal argument, regarding the legitimacy of the message enclosed, is the message itself. The perspectives are paradigm-changing, and the foundations of the enclosed viewpoints have been discovered while not purposefully seeking verification. Yet multiple verifications were received and recorded. They're referenced throughout, or at the end.

If you can't find fault with the messages, consider investigating them further, sharing them, and or living up to them. If you can find fault and can offer argument accordingly, please share. This book seeks truth and wisdom and is written to highlight the significance of certain existential paradigms. It also exists to reawaken long-resting foundational beliefs.

Psychology: All our personal objective perceptions are completely and only subjective. We can only see through one set of eyes, and draw perspectives through the experiences of one being.

Based on that existential law, anyone can dismiss the book's contents, without reason or forethought. The enclosed perspectives, though thoroughly researched and documented, are from a single viewpoint, and you have full right and privilege to accept or ignore.

You're absolutely fine, one way or the other …unless of course, you're dissenting beliefs are hurting people. If your tendency is toward judgment and condemnation, please continue reading. Those actions are the impetus to write this document.

The debated foundational paradigms:
Love vs Hate
Tolerance vs Discrimination
Coexistence vs Annihilation
Equality vs Privilege
Human Advancement vs Antiquated Myopism

...The re-verification or refutation of certain supposedly unarguable longstanding spiritual, cultural, and social beliefs. ... Our paradigms.

This book will offer an awareness of an alternate way to view our reality, which could help some move past the mire we're currently experiencing. We're about to head into the new millennium in one of two ways. We hope all move forward peaceably. Our second option is, not all of us reach the awakening and our planet—our lifeline ... will be worse for wear.

The current dividing point:
Though our species believes we have a significant existence history and certain foundations are old enough to be considered set in stone, humans are actually cosmically young, and certain social institutions perpetuating this inaccuracy are keeping us from advancing as a species.

One such paradigm is religion's unquestioning association with God.
With evaluation, one can conclude: Religion and God aren't necessarily in agreement on many current philosophies, and the disagreement is not difficult to find. Religion is a human institution,

and though it claims to represent God, too many examples exist, showing the opposite to be true.

The argument is: Humans are …human and flawed, and naturally can't exemplify God.

(A few of) The counter-arguments:

- Gender inequality

- Institutional pedophilia. – Not pedophilia alone, which is abhorrent in itself. But the institutional cover-up of the abhorrent act.

- The continual systemic genocide of a naturally occurring type of human, God is quoted as accepting, and who bear no threat to nature, mankind, religion, or God. (LGBT)

- The continual systemic genocide of those with different religious beliefs.

- The inaccurate belief: those of religious authority have the right to murder those not adhering to far less egregious religious 'laws'.

…Failing to reach the top rung of the deity ladder is acceptable. Failure to reach the bottom rung, when claiming to represent God, is not.

Additional differences are throughout the book. There are too many to list here. But please note, this book is not anti-religion.

It just addresses certain spiritual paradigms which have become humanly-influenced and subsequently distorted over time.

On the grandest scale, this planet is the hell or heaven we make it – no prophecy is written in stone. They are shared so we may change course, but changing course is always difficult. This is the garden from which we swear we were removed. We are turning it into a dump. No one else.

**The Message**

This book's message isn't just good news …it's great news, but also unusual. And some information and concepts may shake your soul a bit. It did mine as it was shared, which is a natural reaction when well established, millennia-old paradigms are exposed and subsequently disproven.

Please don't be upset by what you read. The great news - better than the good news of the Bible is: **You are God's**

…and **nothing** can end that or prevent it, and you're more loved and okay than you'll ever understand. …Ever. That is an edict from the Perfect Creator, and His edicts are indisputable. The statement is made in the Bible, but not in the proper universal context. The dynamic is not what you've been led to believe. A detailed explanation will follow.

You need or are requested to do nothing. I'll prove it. You don't suffer whatsoever by rejecting this information. Again, I'll prove it. You're an immortal being. You've already been told that, but in a less than accurate religious paradigm that has somewhat confused you. It's widely believed, humans will either experience eternal heaven or eternal damnation. I'll prove the operational word is *eternal*, then prove the remainder of the statement, false.

There have been wise men who've tried to theorize reincarnation; the idea we're immortal cosmic beings living mortal existences. I will further refine this principle as well.

These concepts will be explained through new and different perspectives, as they were explained (proven) to me. For now though, please conceptualize the idea that some of these new perspectives are nothing but new frameworks of old paradigms …things already spiritually and religiously accepted, though inaccurately, due to the antiquated (non-modern) mindsets of those sharing the original concepts.

# Chapter Two
## GOD Paradigms

**The first lesson**

God is Love. (But not like we've been led to believe)

God is Perfect. (But not like we've been led to believe)

These are longstanding paradigms, but not completely accurate. A human factor has been added that must once again be removed. This is the order these lessons were shared:

**God** is actually: Unconditional **Love/Forgive – One singular concept.**

Our physical understanding of the two separate words is incomplete, but our understanding of the spiritual concept is nonexistent. Our language has no reference or explanation of the encompassing definition of the joined words.

How my personal spiritual experience proving this fact came to pass:

I spend a fair amount of time accessing all information mediums and one day, heard or read something ominous about God; roughly referencing His ability, penchant, seeming joy, cursing and destroying things …SMITING things! (attempt at humor).

I don't remember the actual event or item. That specific information is irrelevant. All I remember is an incessant warning of imminent doom due to our human imperfections, impurity, unholiness, ungodliness, from a supposed religious representative, and going to bed completely unnerved by the never-ending bombardment of impending eternal doom. The gist of my discomfort: The idea almost none of us stand a chance in hell of passing this life *test* and avoiding hell, and if that's what this life and existence is …if that 'reality' is accurate, it is disappointingly insulting to the point of ludicrous – on all physical, emotional, mental-intellectual, and spiritual levels.

I've had a passionate relationship with God for a long time (amazingly good and horrifyingly bad. I'm human). I've read the Bible many times, some parts, incessantly. And one night I seemed to have had enough.

I lie in bed before attempting to sleep, with an attitude of pure disgust toward God…

My thought: *If You (God) are the fucking bastard your religious representatives say you are, you disgust me.*

...which should have retroactively turned me into less than a memory.

I meant the sentence with my heart and soul.

REF: There is no such thing as blasphemy or sacrilege. God is no more offended by your thoughts or actions than you're offended by ants ... or your grandchild if you truly love them. The idea we're an advanced enough life-form to offend spirits is a human over-exaggeration based on a human shortcoming: our seeming self-importance ...but not accurate ...and here's the proof:

There is no time reference between the thought and the following event. It may have happened instantly or occurred later that night, but during my time asleep ...pre-sleep ...not awake, I witnessed three tiny lights come down the wall of my bedroom, enter my right ear, and take me to a place best described as, the brightest black I've ever witnessed.

I was taught one lesson during this event. But not in the way we understand lessons are taught in the physical realm.

While there, I felt a peace and caring, and lack of want for anything, like I've never experienced before or since. It was explained (perfectly) that what was depicted during the earthly religious message that had twisted me so badly regarding God, was the opposite of remotely true, and I ...and everyone - are loved beyond our capacity to comprehend. The love for us is perfect, and there is no flaw or possible chance of change in its continuation. It is how this universe and our existence is set up.

When spiritual entities wish to communicate, they do not struggle, and there's no need for the message to come from outside our being or cross some outer path or plane of existence. The message taught felt like it came to me from within and was infused in me. The message felt like it had suddenly become part of my DNA, though I knew it had just become part of me and wasn't with me before that instant.

But the message was so much more comprehensive. The message was/is multi-tiered, complex in depth, and infinitely encompassing in scope, though simple in concept.

The message: LOVE/FORGIVE ...and how it applies to all aspects of existence.

I was explained/taught how it is the prime rule for all existence; how it is the single rule guiding the spiritual universe, and subsequently the ultimate rule for all existence. And I was taught an amazing aspect of this highest sentient concept:

God *is* this concept and this concept encompasses/epitomizes God – to timeless perfection. There is no flaw in the Being or the Being's ability to continue this edict – without end.

God not only loves and forgives beyond a capacity to comprehend but the concept of LOVE/FORGIVE is the single most important edict/thought/concept in existence. And God is *perfect* at it. And LOVE/FORGIVE the single rule governing the spiritual universe, which is the single beginning and primary universe. And the concept applies to all things, and what each immortal being strives to perfect. The Being who created the rule is perfect at adhering to the rule, because that Being is *perfect*, and that Being is the incarnation of the rule. (more details below regarding *perfect*.)

There is no good place to break the line of thought, so I'm adding the personal amazing aspect, here:

At the moment of my thought, God should have, by all rights and incorrect religious beliefs, retroactively turned me into a non-entity without trace or record of existence. God not only didn't, God instead expressed a level of love beyond comprehension. God instead bothered to share a lesson on who He/She really is, with a creature (me) so below Her ... God lovingly bothered with the equivalent of a cosmic insect, and I to this day am overwhelmed by that level of perfect unconditional love, understanding, and absolute forgiveness.

I expected to die a nasty death that night, and by all previously taught religious axioms, deservedly so, and still struggle to comprehend the level of tender all-encompassing love I was shown. It is inconceivable and incomprehensible.

Another semi-related thought: If you think right about here, that within a few pages, I'm going to dive head first into a mega-preaching Bible-thumping mode – you couldn't be more wrong if you tried. …Instead, I expose Bible sections as fraudulent and point out its failure to adhere to God's primary directive, sometimes using God's own words. Other times, foundational modern beliefs (with extensive bible references) are used. I even attempt to rewrite new perspectives to old stories, using the above single most important maxim in the universe: *Unconditional Love/Forgiveness*.

…Back to the discussion…

But this single lesson wasn't and isn't the only lesson I've received. I've come to realize I've been in communication with the spiritual world for a rather long time, and this ongoing interaction has often been wonderful and awful, but on a less personal level, it's been an eye-opening advent into a different existence perspective, I believe I've been asked to share.

We are loved and protected beyond our ability to comprehend, in all its imagined and even some unimaginable aspects. Our Maker is not only, not the ogre some would have us believe, but is actually this amazingly loving forgiving Being. Why?

God is perfect – and can.

(easy as that)

You are loved for no reason whatsoever.

Convince yourself immediately, there's nothing you can do to change that fact. You can't break God's heart or lose Her love. He demands almost nothing and would like you to understand you're loved for no reason whatsoever. Not something you do or fail to do, but because you exist, and God has the ability.

The lesson shared had a myriad of aspects:

Primarily, you are here to learn and share learning experiences with existence. This is explained in great detail, and ties into every other aspect of existence.

There is no existence exit test (I will offer proof). That's not as ancient a religious belief as you would think and the notion is imperfect, so the notion would be incongruent with a perfect Being.

Not a handful of humans would reach heaven anyway. Yes, most who 'believe' wouldn't reach either, according to certain bible passages. There are multiple passages that make this claim. A few are included in this book, but a specific passage states quite clearly: The *originally written quota* for heaven was 144,000 (Revelations 7: 3-8). We're currently 7.5 BILLION, and countless billions since the first covenant. There are *currently* 1.7 to 2 billion *living* Christians.

(The number entering heaven was believed for centuries …then was suddenly *de-emphasized*. The number once served religion. Religion now realizes the number has become counter-productive.)

Secondly, you wouldn't test your children under those terms. Why would you think God would test you under those terms?

God and certain religions have never met, or met ages ago and have not spoken since, and certain religious principles are for ulterior purposes but have nothing to do with God.

Our words love and forgive are separate in American English. I learned they are one inseparable concept in the spiritual realm. I've also been led to believe, there is no other rule in the spirit universe. I would surmise because a *Perfect* Being has no need to create a second rule, to rule Her realm. Especially since the single rule is perfect. Please notice I do not use 'law'.

Rules connote patience when a being falls short of accomplishment, and offers opportunities to lovingly, patiently address failure and use failure as a measure of effort and persistence, offering an opportunity to express love and patience as the lesser being tries to perfect their adherence.

*Law* doesn't offer the same love, forgiveness, or patience. My message had an emphasis on the concept of *rule*, with the understanding, beings desire to emulate the Creator out of mutual love and discipleship. The *perfect* Being has no need to punish. The Being only teaches and lets existence teach. Her love is complete.

Her patience …infinite. His understanding …perfect. His inclination to punish …nonexistent. (And it's funny, how many humans are offended by the notion.)

We are loved and forgiven beyond our comprehension. Unconditional. Complete. Without fail. Without any inkling of malice by this Being or effort on our part. And we are more alright …more safe …more loved than we can ever comprehend. Nothing can destroy us. Nothing can separate us from this Being. This was part of my message. I am loved and fine, here and after, as are you, as is everyone you love, as is everyone you hate …as are all the creatures floating around this and every other universe. …because the Being CAN …and the Being CAN do whatever She wants. He's PERFECT.

And I start the separation of God and religion here: When I said *you* are loved, I didn't mean you *religious* …you *'believers'*. When I said *you* are God's …I didn't mean you who are good and obedient …or those who go to church …or those who pray …or those who adhere to any other conceived notion of action, condition, or thought …and this will be explained in (wordy) detail below. (More on *PERFECT* in the next section)

Why are we loved without concern for our input?

God can separate our actions from our being, like a grandparent of a very young child. God is cosmically ancient and we are cosmically very young. Look around.

We're also here for no other reason than to experience and learn.

A breakdown of LOVE/FORGIVE:

The two words are separate in our culture and are understood separately. They have separate meanings in American English and no obligatory connection. The two words are not separate in the spiritual universe. Spiritually, they're fused together and cannot be addressed or understood alone. One is impossible without the other. They are one.

**LOVE**

**LOVE**: The spirit-world definition: *Unconditional Love*.

But by definition or action, love isn't unconditional in our physical world. Our society prefers conditional love, and (inaccurately) accepts conditional love as the complete manifestation of the concept. Religions also accept conditional love as their meaning; conditional upon being religious. Contingent on religious conformity.

The best definition of *love* I've ever read is in the Bible. 1 Corinthians 13: 4-8, 13. Please don't read it. I humbly suggest you study it and digest it. Mark it. Write it in a place, easy to access. Cut it out of the book. Tattoo it on your being. Reference it constantly.

Infuse it into your being. Question other concepts in the bible when they disagree with these words, because when they disagree with these words, they disagree with the Being the words represent. …GOD is LOVE. LOVE is GOD.

⁴Love is patient, love is kind. It does not envy, it does not boast, it is not proud. ⁵It does not dishonor others, it is not self-seeking, it is not easily angered, it keeps no record of wrongs. ⁶Love does not delight in evil but rejoices with the truth. ⁷It always protects, always trusts, always hopes, always perseveres. ⁸Love never fails.

GOD is LOVE. Feel free to substitute 'GOD' for 'LOVE' - one word for the other. It's wonderfully true either way.

⁴God is patient, God is kind. God does not envy, God does not boast, God is not proud. ⁵God does not dishonor others, God is not self-seeking, God is not easily angered, and keeps no record of wrongs. ⁶God does not delight in evil but rejoices with the truth. ⁷God always protects, always trusts, always hopes, always perseveres. ⁸God never fails.

Why does the current human definition of *love*, fall short of this definition and its potential?

As individuals, we're taught to strive toward success and witness this love 'reward or denial' action from the people we as children hope offer us nothing but love because they made us. 'Adults' seem to think, by placing stipulations on this most important nonessential, they'll motivate their children.

First, it is an essential life element. This has been proven in orphanage studies (psychology). And the absence of this essential actually costs lives.

Second, conditional love not only is the definition of love most humans offer but the one we were offered when we first understood the definition. And since this is the definition we've learned as young children, we not only hold ourselves and others to this definition but find it difficult to adopt and enforce the accurate definition. (How great would life be if this changed?)

The reason our society has adopted such an unloving expression of love is based on natural human development. Evolution has programmed us to emulate those we trust. We begin life loving unconditionally but reprogram through imitation/modeling as we age. We are perpetuating our own shortcoming.

Secret: Your loved ones will have far more success if they feel unconditionally loved during their lives. You will have a far more successful relationship with them, and you'll experience benefits beyond your current understanding. You'll also come to learn, unconditional love has no negative spiritual ramifications. A perfect Being has made it a perfect concept, and striving toward unconditional love is striving toward a higher existence.

Try this concept unsolicited with any and all your loved ones and watch the reaction you receive. People open unequaled to this level of love, and you begin to receive a new level of love in return, without asking.

The Catch: Success showing unconditional love is difficult for many reasons, including our reprogramming toward conditional love, and our own vulnerability, to mention the most basic. But the success doesn't matter as much as the effort. Only the effort is measured. For the average person, success and effort are almost never positively correlated. Those who've achieved worldly success will argue otherwise, but their opinion is subjective; through a single set of eyes, as previously discussed.

I enjoy contemplating and discussing theory. You'll find most who study psychology, do. I've always had difficulty transforming theory into practical application though, but every once in a while, am able.

The following is an attempt at a practical application of a human perspective on unconditional love:

(What I wish my physical father said to me and had shown me. Please feel free to use it if words fail you, but you're inclined.)

'I love you because you exist. I made you. You are mine and nothing can change that.

I hope you try your best throughout your life and especially when your future is at stake, as it is when you're changing from adolescent to young adult. And know I'll be saddened if I think your effort is less than the effort I feel you have the ability to offer, but I will not be disappointed in you. Your effort is your choice and has nothing to do with my love for you. You can count on that unquestioningly.

But because I love you, please understand my life has told me, your life will be better if you give maximum effort using the gifts you've been given, and prioritize what actions deserve your primary attention. But I understand only 1% fit into the top 1%, and that leaves 99% fitting into the next level down and is divided 99 times. If you try, you can absolutely fail without guilt or remorse. The idea, all it takes is hard work to accomplish what you set out to accomplish, is a lie.

Effort and success are not correlated, no matter how much our culture tells you otherwise. Someone will, I guarantee, be in the bottom 10%. There has always been a bottom 10%. There will always be a bottom 10%. Do not be embarrassed by finding yourself in the bottom 10%. 10% of all people find themselves there, whether temporarily or permanent, by their own actions or actions beyond their control.

But where you fall with regard to achievement has nothing to do with my love for you and how I view you. I'm pleased you are you, and I'm happy with you – always. I'm happy to see you – always. I'm glad you're in my life – always. I love engaging you and being with you, even if we don't share a word together – always. I wish you happiness – always. After you crash and burn, come sit with me and I'll bleed your pain with you – always.

You didn't ask to come into this world. I'm well aware I brought you here without your consent, and this complicated ever-changing world is impossible to keep up with, whether you're an adult or still becoming one. You see my failures and frustrations. I offer you the ability to fail and be frustrated also, because I love you unconditionally.

But because I love you, I wish and hope you'll learn from my bad decisions and experiences. You can avoid some mistakes by learning from my mistakes, though I know your love for me makes you want to imitate me and leads you to believe you'd be more like me if you chose to make your own mistakes, as you know I did.

And if by chance you're not like others …physically, emotionally, mentally, socially, sexually, genderly …your pubic hair is blue, you can see out of your eye tooth …I don't give a fuck. God made you exactly like you are, as She did me, exactly like I am…with a thousand flaws. And you with your flaws were given to me with mine. I brought you here because I wanted to have and love a baby …and you're it …and I love you because you're it …because you exist …including every wart, flaw, and shortcoming.'

(It would be nice, wouldn't it?)

My father was dead a quarter century before I learned the difference between his punishment driven motivational program which included love as a reward, and a discipleship; a love directed modeling based motivational system, as taught by the Christ and the Buddha, for example.

Christ's last command to his disciples (us): "Love one another as I have loved you." John 13:34

Christ's question before asking one of his followers to do something monumental for him:

"Do you love me?"

The precursor question to:

"Then feed my children, and shepherd my sheep." John 21:15

I know a book where the main focus of the entire story culminates in one thought:

'If God is love, then doesn't it only make sense that it is better to love completely wrong than it is to hate completely right?'

(Jake to his mother / Chapter 13 / The Definition of Normal)

Proposed exit test from this earthly life (THE LAST JUDGMENT! …oh no)

If God is love (God is) and can sum the success of your existence into one question (God can) …Which of these two single questions do you hope God asks you?

"Why did you love?"

Or

"Why did you hate?"

[Advice: If you're going to fuck up, pick the fuck-up that most imitates the Ultimate Being asking the question]

What Christ taught about LOVE:

[43] "You have heard it said, 'Love your neighbor and hate your enemy.' [44] But I tell you, love your enemies and pray for those who persecute you, [45] that you may be children of your Father in heaven. [46] If you love those who love you, what reward will you get? Are not even the tax collectors doing that? [47] And if you greet only your own people, what are you doing more than others? Do not even pagans do that?" -The Christ / Matthew 5 **Love for Enemies**

[1]If I speak in the tongues of men and of angels but have not love, I am a noisy gong or a clanging cymbal. [2]And if I have prophetic powers and understand all mysteries and all knowledge, and if I have all faith, so as to remove mountains, but have not love,

I am nothing. ³If I give away all I have, and if I deliver up my body to be burned, but have not love, I gain nothing.  1 Corinthians 13: 1-3

## FORGIVE

¹³ Bear with each other and forgive one another if any of you has a grievance against someone. Forgive as the Lord forgave you. Col 3:13

²¹ Then Peter came to Jesus and asked, "Lord, how many times shall I forgive my brother or sister who sins against me? Up to seven times?" ²² Jesus answered, "I tell you, not seven times, but seventy-seven times.  Mat 18: 21-22

*¹⁴For if you forgive men when they sin against you, your heavenly Father will also forgive you. ¹⁵But if you do not forgive men their sins, your Father will not forgive your sins.  Matthew 6: 14-15*

*²⁵And when you pray, if you hold anything against anyone, forgive him, so that your Father in heaven may forgive you your sins.*  Mark 11: 25

[37] "Do not judge, and you will not be judged. Do not condemn, and you will not be condemned. Forgive, and you will be forgiven. Luke 6: 37

[34]Jesus said, "Father, forgive them, for they do not know what they are doing." Luke 23: 34

*Forgive* is easy to understand without a depth of thought, but holds a far greater meaning with the depth of thought. The contemplated meaning of the spiritual level of *forgiving* has offered new levels of awareness. It is as complicated and deep as the concept of love, and its unconditional meaning, as great as the concept of unconditional love. But the practical application of *forgiving* is much harder than the application of *love.*

(All of these thoughts have been written before, and you're more than welcome to access other examples, books, or definitions, but know I'm well aware these concepts are not original. How could they be? Love/Forgive is an original existence concept. I rewrite their meaning, in an attempt to modernize the explanation and associated thought processes under the premise: Different perspectives of the same material often find different audiences.)

When I contemplated my spiritual advisors' shared spiritual level of these concepts, I realized I was much more comfortable with the aspect of *love*, than *forgive*. I also realized *forgive* is much harder to adhere to. One usually can choose who they love… though an explanation of that limited an application (referenced previously) is offered derogatorily by Christ, in the Christian Bible.

But unlike the limited definition of *love*, *forgive* doesn't offer a selected or pre-chosen group. Everyone is included in the group potentially needing forgiveness, and everyone knows everyone's included. The *forgive* concept is in *The Lord's Prayer*, though religion downplayed its significance by bastardizing the phrase.

Forgive us our *Trespasses* as we forgive others.

*FORGIVE* may be an existence edict with more personal consequences than *LOVE*. Written wisdom throughout time suggests, the offense not forgiven rots the vessel housing it. This means we alone suffer by not forgiving those 'trespassing' us.

Okay, but it's so hard to forgive sometimes, and people seem to be getting worse at forgiving.

Let me help you learn to forgive in the way I've taught myself to be better at the edict, using the following practical application:

When one truly comes to the understanding, God is Perfect, has the ability to address all offenses, and is aware of all things, why worry or wish anyone retribution? It is written, to do so only piles ashes on our own head.

Instead, let the Powers-that-be deal with the ramifications of others' actions. It's not our job or our place, and if our failure to forgive is nothing more than in thought, we contribute nothing toward righting the offense. We gain nothing. Don't compound your injury by injuring yourself too.

Our God and His realm have the power to deal with all who offend us. Let them. God is aware of all happenings, on every level. (If I explained the awareness I've come to learn regarding that thought, you'd get uncomfortable, though the concept is also an old paradigm.) Release your anxiety by realizing God's realm's perfect awareness and power.

In time, you'll come to decide on an even more selfish way to forgive: Pray for those who offend you and disrespect you. Ask God to forgive them. And conversely ...ask forgiveness of those you offend, whether accidentally or on purpose, as quickly as possible, in case they have the ability to let God handle your offense and you suffer the consequences of your actions.

Yes, there are consequences for actions. May God hold you to fewer negative consequences than you've earned.

In time, you'll mature in your forgiving skills and will allow yourself to forgive and release without any of the selfish initial motives. We all have to start somewhere and most of us can't start at the 'expert' level. Most of us have to begin at the 'start' level. It's okay, as long as you start somewhere. And you'll fail often and miserably, but all is forgiven, though we should keep trying every time we fail. Success and effort are not positively correlated. And if God is *Perfect*, the effort counts. (God is. It does.)

Psychology: Don't take offenses personally, especially non-personal offenses, such as being cut off while driving. The person who cuts us off doesn't know us, so why would we take their action personally? Are they ignorant? Maybe. Or maybe they just had a human moment and we're who they had the moment with. We can use the experience for our benefit and decide to assume they're not the asshole we would have declared them before we re-evaluated our own thought process. The more immature the mind, the more offenses 'disrespect'. The more mature, the easier to dismiss the feeling of being disrespected. Yeah, we all get shit on. Welcome to an overcrowded earth.

The psychological theory which helps you forgive:
Understanding Demeanor and the difference between Dispositional vs Situational demeanor
Eastern philosophy regarding understanding demeanor has western philosophy beat, hands down. Eastern philosophy believes: People are inherently good, therefore if someone is displaying a bad

demeanor, they're probably experiencing a situation in their life that's difficult to experience. Western philosophy: He must be an asshole.

Dispositional: 'He or she is probably always miserable or mean' – is almost *never* correct, not to mention, our assumption of this dispositional opinion is rather immature at best, and rather ignorant and dispositionally demeaning at worst. It also contradicts the suppositions of forgiveness and places us further from our goal as maturing humans.

Start preemptively forgiving (forgiveness without internal insult) by dropping assumptions of negative dispositional demeanor, and replacing it with its situational assumption: She's probably going through a difficult experience or situation. I hope she feels better …then learn to take that to its next level: "You look like you're going through a rough patch. Is there anything I can do to help?"

I know an old man who's been ornery and miserable for twenty years and finally became curious enough to break through the coldhearted wall he always seemed to have in place. I asked him sincerely if I could know where his pain came from …and he told me. And his prolonged life situation is beyond any heartache I've ever heard and he's spent thirty years, unable to get over the situation he's been dealt, including no one caring enough to ask if his pain is situational.

We're friends now, and he has dropped his wall. He does things for me now, without asking …just out of kindness. He's one of the sweetest most loveable men I've ever met, but his pain still weighs on him and now on me too, and it's an honor carrying some of it.

I could have enjoyed his friendship for twenty years longer than I'll get to now, for my years of assuming it was his disposition and not his situation causing his demeanor. My loss.

PS: If that someone in *your* life says, "Go away." …don't assume their demeanor is dispositional. They just may not be ready to share their situation.

I over-wrote the word *forgive* using the framework of the word *love* in *The Love Verse* in 1 Corinthians 13: 4-8, 13, and it reads rather interestingly:

Forgiveness is meek. It is the opposite of pride and boastfulness and holds no envy. It honors others. It is the opposite of self-seeking, the opposite of anger and evil. It keeps no record of wrongs. Forgiveness is above justice. It always trusts, always hopes, always perseveres. Forgiveness feeds love, and never fails love.

And takes more strength than any action known to man.

What Christ said about *Forgive* :
Matthew 6:

¹⁴ For if you forgive other people when they sin against you, your heavenly Father will also forgive you.

We're human. Shouldn't we forgive others for being human ...for being different ...for being less than our definition of what they should be, as we hope they forgive us when we're less than they expect or deserve? (not a new concept)

**LOVE/FORGIVE   as a single concept:**
The highest degree of existence. Perfect. Not only does the Creator qualify, but God is the incarnation and the model. The ability to love/forgive unconditionally and in the purest form eliminates all flaws and exists above all faults. This includes all misidentifiers mentioned in all antiquated religious books, written during antiquated times, in antiquated places, by humans with less than advanced awareness.

Human attempts at application:
Being constantly accepting of human imperfections and differences; empathy and understanding, caring, courteousness, trusting existence and the Being that made it. Recognizing instantly and continuously that we're spiritually all brothers and sisters ...always.

All mature beings desire to be honorable, wanting nothing more than peace, harmony, an opportunity to survive, if not thrive …to grow. Everyone around the world reveres family, friends, hopes for peace, and values life. When one visits other places around the world, one finds there are no differences between us. We all hope, dream, and have aspirations for a better world.

What is not to love and forgive if we all gain selfishly and personally by doing so? Will working toward love/forgive, or doing the opposite, cause harmony or chaos? Will finding and magnifying our differences make us safer or place our existence in peril? Will radicalizing our beliefs exemplify our Teacher or bastardize God's message?

Is win/lose really necessary or only childish?

Unconditional love can only be attained after unconditional forgiveness is offered. Unconditional forgiveness can only be attained after unconditional love is given. Will we ever be good at it? The result isn't as concerning as the effort.

Start small. Start with you. Be patient. Be relentless in your effort, but expect to fail before you succeed. And know that's normal.

"The weak can never forgive. Forgiveness is the attribute of the strong." – Mahatma Gandhi

"You more than anyone, deserve your unconditional love and forgiveness." – Siddhartha Gautama.

"To understand everything is to forgive everything."

– Madame de Stael – (Proverb?)

# Chapter Three
## Perfect

**God is Perfect (But not like we've been led to believe)**

[48] Be perfect, therefore, as your heavenly Father is perfect.

Mat 5: 48 / The Christ's Sermon on the Mount / Love for Enemies

When the *other realm* event happened, I obviously had an instant revision of the religious/archetypical description of God and the definition of *perfect*. I had just been shown a level of *perfection* I had no idea existed and felt a need to revisit the differences in paradigms which have existed for thousands of years, and the new awareness which had been explained so infusingly inside me.

My first revelation after the event was euphoria. I just found out God is the *perfect* I had always fantasized and not the demon ogre our 'good book' or preachers portray. I was just informed we all go to 'heaven' (the spiritual universe) after we die and everyone we love has gone there or will go there, and is completely okay. They are loved and forgiven like a perfect Being can.

I immediately began trying to put into words … trying to describe the euphoria felt by the level of perfect love/forgiveness I had just received, enjoyed, and benefitted from, and years later, still struggle to describe the depth of love and caring I felt. And though

I've written fifty thousand words trying to describe the experience in human terms, the best way to describe the experience and subsequent feeling is with one word, and it's the word Christ used above: *Perfect.*

Do not dismiss the word. Please contemplate it.

*Perfect*

Contemplate what specifics would be in your definition. Then realize, no matter how your imagination differs from what you've been requested to believe, your imagination is more accurate than are our social and religious paradigms regarding *perfect*, as it pertains to the Perfect Being.

Religion has diluted …bastardized the word and their foundational reasoning is the bastardization of the word in the Bible.

I don't believe this inaccuracy was done to deceive or harm. I've been explained the difference between pure perfection and the antiquated dogmatic human definition, and for all the things I wish to share, this difference is the second most important idea within this document.

There are two definitions of *perfect*. Most aren't aware, because there shouldn't be two definitions. Allow me to describe first, the imperfect antiquated dogmatic definition, then I'll describe the definition that is worthy of a Being who loves and forgives beyond your wildest imagination.

The dogmatic definition of a perfect God:

He is jealous, easy to anger, constantly disappointed, vindictive, trite, pompous, insistent, temperamental, and completely overbearing.   You know …but perfect.

God's first interaction with humans was to curse the entire species in perpetuity because one human bit a fruit after He spitefully placed it on the prettiest tree in the center of our garden. One of his next interactions was to flood and kill all but two of the entire species because they were being impure … 'human'.

He cursed every individual ethnicity of humans except Israelites and He treats that group like trash; constantly allowing them to be run over by all their enemies, who he hates, solely because the Israelites were acting less than holy/pure. And He continuously makes, then especially hates LGBT.

He killed 42 teenagers by having them mauled by bears, for calling a bald person, 'baldy'. (Elisha - 2 Kings 2:23-24) Then he wants to claim he loves us by torturing his only son and subjecting him to one of the most grueling gruesome deaths known to man. He also not only has declared an exit test but has decreed, almost none of us will pass and the penalty for not passing is a level of pure fucking evil beyond description …eternal damnation.

(If _THIS_ is how perfect your god is, your god is a perfect prize and a half)

PERFECT (the *perfect* PERFECT):

Take a moment and picture what characteristics you'd like to see and would hope you receive, from a Being who made you exactly how you are and who you are. What would you hope they expect from you …offer you, given who you know you are? Think …would they not only be okay with your imperfections but patient and caring to a fault …understanding and empathetic to your minutest problem and concern …forgiving when you make mistakes …always going past offering you the benefit of the doubt …immeasurably slow and patient when teaching …forgiving before you ask, no matter how big your errors …using every opportunity to teach, and taking as long as necessary for you to learn…even if the teaching/learning process took a thousand …ten thousand lifetimes? …Shares messages you're loved, even when you feel you don't deserve love? Have a loving plan and place for you, everyone you love, and everyone He's created – for all eternity?

Would the Being know your heart and even if you fucked up completely, be able to see deep into your soul, and understand all the complex reasons why? And give you another opportunity to make a better decision, even if that opportunity can't come during this current lifetime? What if it took one thousand times before you learned to make a better decision? Would you like to believe a perfect Being who's existed a <u>minimum</u> of 14 billion years (if He came into existence the day He created this universe) would offer you a thousand chances? …Ten thousand? A million?

And when you learn, celebrate your breakthrough with you and be pleased with your growth? ...Just consider you Her child, and just love you whether you succeed or fail? I mean, truly love you ...forever ...no deed needing to be accomplished by you ...no judgment ...just pure perfect never-ending 'you're mine and not a fucking thing in heaven or hell can change that', unconditional love.

Guess what? I didn't make that up. I'm not bright enough. That message was shared with me ...infused into me. You're so okay and so loved, you as an imperfect being experiencing the pushes and pulls of existence, are loved and cared for beyond your wildest imagination, by a Being so perfect, you can't write the things you hope this Being is, and encompass how perfect this Being is. If you think what YOUR definition of perfect would entail, it could never fully describe how perfect the Being is and how perfectly you're cared for ...protected ...guaranteed an existence beyond your wildest imagination, communing with beings you can't fathom ...seeing ...experiencing things more wondrous than you can envision. Perfect in a perfect way. Perfect in demeanor. No anger. No animosity. No exit test. No judgment. Only unconditional love.

And you don't have to do a thing to receive this. In fact, it has been stated in ancient books and beliefs, including the Bible: ***You can't earn it.***

What you have *not* been told is: ***You already own it.***

(this last point is discussed in great great detail below)

No, you don't have to find God. She doesn't play hide-n-seek. No, you don't have to claim Christ is God. Remember the rule: **You *cannot* earn it.** In scholastic terms, that means there's *nothing* you can do. In religious terms, that means you have to *believe*. What religion didn't comprehend when it was established is: *Believing* is a conscious act, and if that's the requisite, we would then be *earning* our salvation, so in essence, religion contradicts their own reasoning behind their primary edict. At least they got the first half of the edict right.

The spiritual world doesn't have the pushes and pulls of physical existence. There's nothing life-threatening. There are no desires, needs, cravings, yearnings to attract or tempt, or fears, doubts, worries, terrors, dreads to repel or threaten you.

There are no earthly/physical needs or wants, no desire for power, riches, fame, beauty. But there is an all-encompassing feeling of love. A feeling, you're inside the love. It surrounds you. It touches you softly…intensely…perfectly. It's complete. It's perfect.

This is how God is perfect now as She was before time began. This is why He will not change.

Does it confuse you then, why shit happens? Earth shit happens. Physical universe shit happens. Yes, I'll explain why like I was explained why. No, none of the events, whether personal or societal, are punishment based on impatience, frustration, disappointment; nothing a *sign of God's wrathful anger.*

That opinion is antiquated religious teachings loaded with conclusions based on transductive reasoning, mired in time/place foundations, and a subject for another dissertation.

Some of God's *tyrant traits* are human misinterpretations. Others are attempts to help govern; to keep an earthly group of not yet mature humans under control, with the threat of an ultimate punisher. (And still, we have atrocities). These concepts fail because they're a set of edicts based on laws instead of love, though the laws are supposedly based on love. But it's easy to see through hollow words of love.

A Being older than the universe, impatient? Mad at us for being human? You can make up lies giving examples but you can't make an argument for it.

God put a tree in the middle of a garden with the best fruit on the planet, then got mad some lady ate a piece? How about, placed a tree in the middle of a garden **_SO_** humans would eat the fruit and become sentient; become God's children?

Which point-of-view sounds perfect and which sounds like an author didn't quite understand what he didn't understand, and wrote what he didn't quite understand, using his limited worldliness based on his time and place of existence?

Did you notice the amazing difficulty trying to put my experience with God's spiritual universe, into words? The difficulty I experienced describing true perfect and the accompanying bliss? I've been trying to do it for ten years, and I always feel I fail. I literally am lost for the words to explain the feeling … the lessons. I fail and forgive the tribesmen two-thousand years ago who also failed to grasp the concept of *perfect*. I know God forgives them. They tried. They didn't succeed, and I understand why. Physical experiences get in the way.

Another quick try…

You are an immortal creature. God makes nothing temporary. Think about it. Why would He be bothered? You are living a mortal life, so you may experience the pushes and pulls of the mortal existence you're being shown, for reasons I'll explain. The great news: There is no experience in this physical universe which harms your immortal existence. There is no perpetual damnation. There is no exit test. **THERE IS NO HELL.**

(Yeah, I screamed it. It needs to be screamed from mountaintops. It's one of the sickest lies humans perpetuate.)

The Great Flood:

The world flooded and there is written evidence many survived around the world. It's in this document. But God didn't flood Earth because He's an unforgiving unpleasant ogre. It happened naturally, and this idea God is not only that hands-on, but He's hands-on because He's continually disgusted with us, is an inaccuracy which needs addressing.

But it's paradigm-shifting intellectual discussions like this, that I expect to catch hell for. I'm going to expose the difference between perfect and Bible/religious 'perfect' and I know the shit I'm going to receive by the exercise. But this is necessary because the bible/religious definition of perfect is fucking up a lot of God's children …my brothers and sisters …and watching idly without action isn't acceptable, even at personal risk.

My revelation was also life-altering to the point of unnerving, because, after being explained, and experiencing what true perfection is, I had a hard time figuring out:

1. How religion and God had grown so apart.
2. Why God would allow the organizations that supposedly represent Him, to misrepresent Her so distastefully.

I have not been brought back to the spirit realm for those answers, but the explanations and answers keep coming. The two points are discussed below and are secondary points to the discussion on *perfect*.

Another way to share a new definition of *perfect* is to reference something written much closer to the *other realm event*. The original excerpt dealing directly with the difference between the dogmatic definition and actual definition of *perfect* is below. I like to believe I'm a better writer now, but there was an overwhelming residual euphoria when I originally wrote the discussion. The *other realm event* was just months past, and I needed to share the experience. I needed to shout what I was feeling, though I now feel I didn't express it well enough after reading back on it. It needs expanding, and re-shouting, and that's what I'm doing now…

The (Definition of Perfect) discussion between Jake and his Christian institution educated mother / Chapter 13 / The Definition of Normal

I …

"…God first."

He welcomed her choice. "I agree. He is first. He's perfect, don't you agree?"

"Yes." Her eyes narrowed.

He smiled and continued. "What's your definition of perfect?"

She held her sandwich as she rested her hand on her plate. "I don't know. We were taught He's perfect."

He also lowered his sandwich to just above his plate. "Can He get angry?"

She smiled. "Hell yeah."

"Does He ever hate? Does He ever take sides?"

Her breathing increased again, and she smiled. "Some of the stories seem like it, sure."

"Some of the stories do seem like it, don't they?" He thought about those words for a second and inhaled. "May I expand on the popular dogmatic version of perfect?" She nodded and he continued. "Perfect, the typical two-thousand-year-old dogmatic view taught in some of our finer institutions is, the perfect God has some interesting human qualities, including jealousy, anger, frustration, impatience, even though they acknowledge his perfection. Certain well accepted mainline stories have God creating us and almost immediately being disappointed in us and telling us we can't be in heaven with Him without outside intervention. He is more often than not, dissatisfied with us, and very few get to be on His good side, especially if you're human."

He stared at her before continuing. "Is it okay if that's not my definition of perfect? Is it okay if I share *my* definition of what I perceive is the definition of a perfect God?"

She looked at him curiously. "Sure."

He tilted his head and offered a half smirk. "My definition of perfect is without flaw in every and any action. He loves perfectly. By definition…unconditionally. That means He's never angry or dissatisfied with us. He made us human, which means He has no problem with us being human. Seems silly to think otherwise, doesn't it? Dad loves me even though I'm human. Dad doesn't have a problem I'm human. Do you mean to tell me God could take a lesson from dad? Or is God perfect at it?" He paused and eyed her for a reaction to anything so far. She offered none, so he continued. "He forgives perfectly. Dad forgives me for being an idiot and dad isn't perfect. How could dad be better at it than God?" He paused and they both took a bite of their sandwiches. "Do you and dad have intentions of someday leaving me this house?"

She sat up, pleasantly surprised by the change in topic. "Of course. Do you think you'd ever live here?"

He breathed in. "Do you think God would make a house for us and not have us live in it? Do you think He wants us to but doesn't always get His way? How about not make enough room for us when a universe of rooms take nothing more than a fleeting thought, the room He has to work with is the entire spiritual universe and no one takes up any room? Not my definition of perfect. Yours?"

Her reply was emotionless. "No."

"I know this is going to sound weird, but I thought of something God can't do."

She smiled at his strange statement and waited with a look of curiosity.

"He can't do anything not perfectly. And you know what that eliminates?" He paused and smiled. "Every childish human emotion. Hate, anger, jealousy, pettiness…all of them. It seems the dogmatic and human definition of perfect has the flaws humans have. How funny is that?"

She quietly looked at his face and shoulders and sighed. Her non-reply caused him to wonder if she was hearing him, but he had to continue. He straightened the chips on his plate, then picked one up. Her stare caught him off guard. "Is it okay to go on?"

She nodded, "Yes."

He paused and looked at her to confirm her reply, then continued. "Do you think anything so perfect would ever create something He wasn't aware He was creating? How about something He disliked? He can create anything, any way He wants. Could He really be bothered creating something that offended Him? Or is He flawed? Or are we too stupid to realize He's not flawed?" ]

…

God isn't flawed, nor would He create something just to destroy it. Nothing can challenge God, so there would be no satisfaction in the destruction, but God creating something just so She could destroy it would also show God to be less than perfect. Is God perfect or not?

Certain organizations swear God is perfect, then offer examples and explanations of the pettiest uncaring imperfect Being imaginable. Do the organizations not hear their own words? Are religious organizations contemplating what they're saying?

Argument: But God's so pure, perfect, and divine, She's unapproachably above our puny impure souls.

There is no such thing as impure human souls. It's a middle-eastern / Puritanical concept. We are what we are; new sentient animals feeling our way through our beginning (pre- self-annihilation) years. Nothing is impure about us or our struggles. Childish, immature, self-aggrandizing, self-important, selfish, self-centered, self-serving, vain …but not spiritually impure.

As for unapproachable: Us calling God: 'Father' – is discussed later.

God *is* just a loving creator and not the surly ogre certain stories make God out to be. The authors of those stories didn't transcend time and place. Those perspectives come exactly from their time and place. There's proof, and it's shared.

Yes, if God is perfect, you should have questions that need explaining. So did I. Amazingly, they were explained, and they're in this book.

SIDE NOTE: From what I am led to believe, God strikes very few things dead, or She would have destroyed the angels who betrayed Him, and God didn't. They exist, and I'm pretty sure they're rather active on this planet, due to, or proven by a certain unexplained hatred permeating many humans.

As mentioned prior, nothing can hurt our immortal beings; not even these angels. But these angels can affect our human course-of-events. They feed hate and feed off hate.

TO ALL CURRENT 'CHILDREN OF GOD' who hate in God's name:

If you think certain humans, such as LGBT are a mistake. See the notes on **_PERFECT_**. God is aware of and approves of everything She creates. And if by chance God is *still* creating things humans have tried to eradicate for *centuries,* and certain people *still* exist in every corner of the world, then maybe they don't exist in *spite* of God, but instead exist *because* of God, in *spite* of religion, and antiquated social paradigms.

Now, if you're a hater, remove the word 'maybe' and read the sentence until the idea becomes part of your being, right after you contemplate exactly how perfect your God is, and how imperfect, human perception is …no matter how old the paradigm …no matter who perpetuates the inaccurate belief.

I offer an experience below that is an eye-opening practical application to this paradigm-altering concept. I have also received the idea that this lgbt/religion conflict is a test for the religious …and there are excerpts from the bible that back this premise, which I share below.

SECRET: It's not what goes in your mouth that makes you good or bad, but what comes out of your mouth.

[18] "And He said to them, "Are you so lacking in understanding also? Don't you understand that whatever goes into the man from outside cannot defile him? [19] For it doesn't go into their heart but into their stomach, and then out of the body. [20] What comes out of a person is what defiles them. [21] For it is from within, from a person's heart, that evil thoughts come—greed, malice, deceit, envy, slander, arrogance and folly. [23] All these evils come from inside and defile a person." Mark 7: 18-23

Yes, we're well below God in all things. Yes, we're imperfect and God is perfect. But we don't have to be quite as imperfect as we're volunteering at the moment.

To those who hate:

"A new command I give you: Love one another. As I have loved you, so you must love one another. By this everyone will know you are my disciples, if you love one another" (Christ's words) John 13: 34-35 (I plan on repeating that.)

"Our job is to love others without stopping to inquire whether or not they are worthy." – Siddhartha Gautama (Buddha)

Two of the most impressive people ever to walk the face of the earth offered the same message. Maybe we should give their message a try. Maybe we're being given the ultimatum to do so.

And the Lord separated the sheep and goats, and one group turned to Him, "But Lord, you know us and we know you." And the Lord replied, "Go away. I do not recognize you."

**The idea: "You're not 'saved' unless you find God and profess Him God."** (God's supposed need for us to find Him.)

Likened to a game of Hide and Seek

A child and adult decide to play hide-and-seek in a house and the adult sets a single rule: The child is not allowed outside. Then as the child counts, the adult exits the house.

Would the adult expect the child to find him? Would the adult be mad if the child didn't find him? Would the adult punish the child for not finding him?

God confined all physical beings <u>of</u> this universe – <u>to</u> this universe, but God left this universe, with the strict understanding: if we don't find Him, we're in trouble and will be punished?

Not my definition of perfect …and God is perfect.

You don't have to find Him. God is God whether we acknowledge Her as such, or not. We're God's children because God is perfect and made us His children; not because we find Him or do any other physical, mental, social or emotional act. We're here to experience existence and to learn from the experiences. God is not playing hide-and-seek with us.

We're just here to learn. In some lifetimes, we'll know God exists. In some lifetimes, we won't. In some lifetimes you'll love God. In some lifetimes you will hate the Being. In some, you'll be blessed. In some, you'll feel you've been cursed. In some lifetimes you and God will ignore each other completely (Ecclesiastes). But we will always learn …always experience. We'll always be moving toward a relationship with the Perfect Being, as sentient beings who understand more and more existence, growing closer to communing with like beings, ready to enjoy all existence in all its majestic manifestations.

God made our universe with one simple non-breakable rule: As physical beings (while we're alive) we do not have the ability to leave the physical universe under our own volition …but God does and did.

And someone has convinced us it's imperative to find God? …And convinced us, God is somehow offended and we're not His if we don't?

Religion, however, has a high stake in convincing us we need to find God, and the only way to do so is through their specific religious organization …with physical obligations, of course.

**The idea God demands we worship Her:**

Do you need homage from ants?

Do we demand ants worship humans? Are we the superior species on the planet? How come we don't demand other species worship us? If they did have the ability, what would be our gain by being worshipped?

If being worshipped is a command of God, why would God feel the need to be worshipped? What would be His gain by being worshipped? Does His proposed need to be worshipped show a weakness or flaw in God's psyche? …a flaw in His perfection?

If you were the single being who created and ruled universes, would you feel the need to be worshipped or would you recognize your place in all existence, whether worshipped or not? Would you feel the need to separate lower life-forms between those who worship you and those who don't? Remember, you're so far above any other life-form, they are but ants to you.

My definition of perfect eliminates God's supposed demand to be worshipped. Religion disagrees, but they seem to have a financial incentive to disagree, which makes their opinion invalid in my humble opinion.

Quote: Never take the advice of anyone who stands to gain financially from it. –

Last note on *Perfect*:

Yes, I promise I'll explain things that seem far from perfect. Yes, there's a legitimate explanation (mentioned in passing above). Yes, you'll get it when it's explained with more detail. Yes, I get what you're questioning, especially those who have gone through tremendous heartache, tremendous loss, tremendous confusion. Yes, it will make sense. Yes, the explanation may not be what you want to hear. …Neither was the experience. You'll understand the explanation just the same.

Understand one simple concept from this entire diatribe: Our God is more perfect than we could ever fathom, and it will take us a million lifetimes before we understand the depths of this perfect perfect wonderful loving forgiving Being.

Everything you can think. Everything you can hope.

If you think: "But a perfect loving Mother would have this trait, or be that." …yes.

"…And I wouldn't have to worry about this and I wouldn't have to do that …and my baby and grandma are in heaven and there's no exit test or hell …and we're really alright? Really?"

Yes.


"Commandments": Middle-eastern perspectives influenced by American Puritanism which sounds like four-year-olds telling their younger siblings…. "Mommy said you have to do this and this, and don't touch that, or you'll be in big trouble."

…instead…

God's Rules:

I picture a loving God saying, "These are rules I'd love you to learn to live by. They will serve you and your entire world. Do you see how I love you? Love your brothers and sisters the same way. Will you be perfect at it? No, but don't stop trying. I'll be patient, but request you keep trying. And you're going to have rough days, weeks, years, lives, and I'll ignore them. But I want you to notice me smiling and loving you on your bad ones, and then I want you to try again.

Will you have extreme screw-ups? Yes. You're human and I invented human, so I know what they are and what they look like. And you'll get scolded every once in a while, and the universe you live in has its own natural imperfections. They'll feel like scoldings too, but they're not. Everything is laid out for you to learn. But know I love you and nothing can harm you because I'm perfect, this is what I wish, and I get my wishes."

Am I allowed to think what I'd wish my God would say or who I wish my God could be? Yes. I'm God's child. God wants me to emulate Him …like a human parent wants of their child. May I ask, "Dad, do you do this?" "Dad, am I supposed to do it that way …say it that way?"

And a perfect father would say, "Yes, child. Watch me. Did you see how I did that …said that?"

(Can you fathom – *Perfect* ?)

Do you think people know what *modeling* is but God doesn't? Do you think He edicts/ asks/demands we Love/Forgive, but He doesn't, or can't, or won't?

Or is God *perfect* at it?

**The Disconnect between a perfect God and Religion's imperfect interpretation of God**

Now that I've established the argument regarding a Perfect Creator, including the argument's foundation: Love/Forgive, I would like to address the cognitive dissonance between my perspective and existing paradigms.

The original two points: If God is perfect, why…
1. …have religions grown so apart from the true understanding of who God is?
2. …would God allow the organizations that supposedly represent Him, to misrepresent Her so distastefully?

The first point is easy to comprehend. It is complicated but easy. The second point has been a great lesson; an almost overwhelming lesson, involving revelations beyond what I had ever previously thought.

Point 1:

Control. One can argue why religion was created or what its intent was, but understand who the humans were who finalized organized religion. And if you think they were pure-hearted, with concern for humanity's best interests, read more. These people had mentalities befitting their first-century existence, and the law of the day was feudalism. Stories of Kings like Arthur are wonderful …fiction.

The portrayal of an unapproachable, rather ominous God was created mainly to herd and control the kingdom population. It also fit Emperor Constantine's geographic and population diversification concerns and subsequent needs. It fit the mindset of the time and place, -1st century CE- and other empty governance holes in that society, but the one concept the organizers weren't concerned with, is the truth.

Whether they could fathom the truth, is topic for a different discussion. Remember, they didn't know where the Sun went at night, or that the (believed—flat) earth, which everything revolved around, wasn't the only celestial planet in the universe (Copernicus didn't offer his heliocentric theory until 1543 CE. The 1st galaxy outside the Milky Way wasn't discovered until 1930).

The truth just didn't fit anyone's abilities, needs, or concerns at the time and there has never been a good time to reset for accuracy. Roughly twenty percent of our current society still doesn't feel the need to discover the truth or that it's time to reset for accuracy, two *thousand* years later.

No God isn't unapproachable, or She wouldn't have bothered with me after my thought. God would have just struck me dead, and existence would have retroactively wiped me from memory.

Yes, it *seems* like God is unapproachable. He is a Being so great, we cannot handle Her awe and presence, even for a fleeting nanosecond. That doesn't mean we can't interact. That doesn't mean God doesn't allow interaction. That doesn't mean God can't or won't interact. Quite the opposite. God does interact, but it's awful when God does, and God knows it's awful. No, not the colloquial awful; the literal awful. So full of awe it is overwhelming and hard for us to handle. ...Almost impossible, actually.

And if you're religious and really believe God isn't approachable, why do you pray to him and call him Father? And why did He supposedly ask you to call Him Father? Christ calls him Abba, which translates to 'daddy'. (How perfect is a God who creates universes for fun and then tells us it's okay to call him *Dad*?)

Point 2

This existence is a learning process and God seems to let his children play out their own learning process because existence is a learning tool, based on experiences. God doesn't interfere, even for self-annihilations. It has been explained to me, we're immortal. Gautama talked extensively about reincarnation, and so did Christ, though Constantine didn't like the theory and removed all but one veiled reference from the Bible. He didn't leave it on purpose. It's cryptic and religion missed it because they don't understand it.

I've been explained why reincarnation is real. I believe the explanation clarifies its legitimacy. It is explained later because the explanation would take the current topic too far off topic.

Why God doesn't have a problem with us being so far off course, regarding who He is: Life is an ongoing learning process and we're here primarily to learn, secondarily, to feed consciousness with reactions to experiences, whether our own or situations thrust upon us. But since nothing can destroy our immortal beings …God has no need to intervene as a corrective agent. He is more inclined to do just the opposite. It serves the greater cosmic consciousness to let even the extreme play out.

Then why am I sharing this? Because I'm not God, and the extreme is getting …extreme. The hatred is getting extreme, but the social scenarios always seem to offer amazing lessons for those involved.

# Chapter Four
## Love versus Hate

Hatred does not cease by hatred, but only by love; this is the eternal rule. – Buddha

During a recent summer, I received notification a specific religious group would be visiting the city I reside near, to demean the LGBT people going into a certain building.

(Yes, I'm afraid to give details. The organization seems to take legal action whenever possible. It can be a financial resource method.)

And people were organizing, in the hope of standing between these visitors and those needing access to the building.

I had recently adopted the LGBT equality cause, though I've always had a strong compulsion to fight inequality and injustice on any and every level. I'm as adamant about equality in all other manifestations, but this specific event coincided with incidents which were currently relevant in my life.

With the fear, the human turn-out would fall well short of separating the two groups, I decided to be one more soul who would spend a summer weekday with the others who show up.

To everyone's surprise, far more people showed up willing to stand between these two groups, than anyone anticipated. The organizers had nicknamed the group: The Wall of Love. I was one of the people in The Wall of Love. And for my experiences …my lessons… I noticed something astoundingly remarkable during the event:

Many in the wall of love, were what the middle of our society would call, the fringe…the edge of society. Many of us had physical looks that easily identified us as anything but 'middle of society normal'. I won't describe those occupying the wall of love, in detail, but for those without good imagination, I'll offer some general observations: More atypical colors and styles of hair than I've ever seen. More tattoos. Clothing like nothing in the stores I shop. Clothing worn outside their typically assigned gender groups. More metal piercing skin than adorning necks, wrists, and fingers. …I'm sure you get the idea.

Many of these people inside the wall of love were holding signs, making fun of the religion and god the visiting organization represented. Many signs projected a cold finality while displaying extreme messages against god and the religion representing this god.

I noted:

One group had come to share a message of condemnation, under the premise, their message came from their creator and his sole reference book and held the authority of the creators' commanded religious beliefs.

And one group of seemingly godless misfits standing in direct line of the condemnation, protecting …guarding …taking the brunt of the abusive insults, in order to separate the innocents who needed to visit the facility, and those targeting the innocent with hatred. The wall participants were mostly strangers, but the instant camaraderie was not only noticed, it could also be felt, and among their commonalities was a refusal to accept this god's perceived level of condemnation normality; declaring god a fraud at best, and a heartless demon at worst.

What I saw:

One group hating in the supposed name of God, and the other loving, in the face of …in spite of …against the demand of this supposed creator being.

And I realized this existence is a test:

LOVE versus HATE


And the funny part is: In modern human perception - righteousness, religion, and supposedly God have been and are currently on the HATE side. And the freaks, the dregs, the tortured fringe of society were on the LOVE side, while telling God and His religion to go fuck themselves. It was amusing how blunt the message was.

I stood in the middle of this event – tickled inside! I was witnessing an awareness beyond my human scope.

And I realized: If you decide to love – *against* the tyrant ogre that is this seemingly unbending god of antiquated religions …If you can love when all that is righteous, including God, says you should hate …you pass God's ultimate test!! YOU WIN! YOU GET IT! YOU GOT IT! YOU'RE GOOD!

(Remember God's last command: John 13: 34-35)

And those who thought they were carrying out God's message and will as Her children were falling way short of God's primary directive and by no means representing God …and those sure they were defying God by loving their kin, the fringe and those naturally born different – were doing EXACTLY what God's children are requested to do. And I stood in amazement …in pure wonderment. The more I contemplated this drama playing out around me, the more in awe I was to have witnessed this interaction.

The 'Wall' people left their routines and lives, for one day …anonymously …at cost …for no reward …guaranteed no personal gain or recognition …and protected strangers they never met and would never know …for no other reason than, these strangers needed love and protection.

And there were an estimated few thousand 'wall people'. So many, that when the religious group showed up, half of us didn't know they were there. We were *that* separated.

There were so many 'wall people', the organizers had to draw chalk lines on the ground so the path into the building remained passable. And they stayed longer than needed …on a hotter-than-hell day in an inner-city. One teenager, barely old enough to drive, drove ten hours to stand anonymously and love anonymously. I watched a Buddhist monk and Catholic priest stand together in love and camaraderie, inside the wall with the supposed godless.

Who are God's children? Let me repeat the lines I'll repeat all too often throughout this document: "Love one another as I have loved you. By this they will know you are my disciples, if you love one another." John 13 34-35 (If you need the definition of love again, it's in 1 Cor 13: 4-8, 13)

[9] Anyone who claims to be in the light but hates a brother or sister is still in the darkness. [10] Anyone who loves their brother and sister lives in the light, and there is nothing in them to make them stumble. [11] But anyone who hates a brother or sister is in the darkness and walks around in the darkness." John 2: 9-11

(Spiritual light and spiritual darkness)

The counter-argument: Yeah, but they're the religious extreme.

No, they're not. Their actions are extreme, but their mindset is more accepted than condemned by mainstream religious. Mainstream religion is teaching, hate and exclusion are acceptable. They just keep their hatred somewhat muted. The hatred is equal. The unacceptance is equal. The exclusion is equal, or religion and the religious would have condemned hatred and exclusion by now …and they haven't.

So what is God's relationship with the fringe, the supposed dregs, the cast-offs; those naturally born different? Those who have been so abused by their birthright, they curse the God who made them?

God is as far above us as certain groups think, but not in the way these groups portray the distance. God understands what lessons are being given to whom, and to understand everything is to forgive everything.

Each individual is exactly what God intended to make. He makes *NO* mistakes. He does, however, make things and circumstances to teach us. Not to trip us or test us …to *teach* us. We are given lessons and often, that means we must experience something many do not. And often, that's done by making us something others are not.

But at no time does God not love us; every pathetic soul. God also isn't as concerned with our petty offenses as some would like to believe and profess, and that includes both sides of the measure. Yes, God even loves the religious haters.

Don't be confused by what you've been told. Just look at the offenses of those currently explaining the perceived religious laws, and realize God in His perfection, doesn't offend easily (or at all). Nothing is God's equal, and us offending Him would be equivalent to humans being offended by ants.

And God lets the actions play out, and the lessons that are taught are more a gift than we'll ever understand. They help us become the immortal beings we hope to become.

There is an excerpt in a book, as two (supposedly) fringe humans are out in public trying to innocently enjoy a harmless shopping excursion, as is typical and normal, but their activity is interrupted by a stranger's demeaning stare.

...

[ ...Stephanie felt like an older sister, disheartened for her sibling, by the fleeting, demeaning event. "Are you okay with that?" She gave Colleen the slightest head gesture toward the counter behind them. Sharing yet another uninvited experience in an existence where the lessons are either overabundant or nonexistent.
–*The Definition of Equal*    ]

...

He who learns must suffer, and even in our sleep, pain that cannot forget falls drop by drop upon the heart. And in our own despair, against our will, comes wisdom to us by the awful grace of God. – Aeschylus

The lessons individuals receive on this planet are either overabundant or close to non-existent. The fringe are included in the overabundant group. They know what real love looks like because they experience hate and love in a way, average people never fathom. They receive exclusion and inclusion in the same manner …heartache, failure, loss, unfortunate circumstances, for no other reason than who and how they were made …an excess of experiences, while others march through this existence without a handful of lessons. One group swearing they've mastered existence; one sure they've failed at every turn, including their birthright.

"He who learns must suffer…" The saying is thousands of years old and written by a genius whose realizations have transcended time. Know, his words only confirm his receipt of the lessons he received.

The lesson on view that hot summer day:
Can you love in spite of all the righteous, proper, in-good-standing, and acceptable cultural and societal edicts to hate? Can

you defy even the consensus's God, and love against all good sense and argument? Against God Himself?

Many of those who can and do show this ability to love, have come to dismiss the God they suppose is behind the hate edicts. But nothing pleases God more than those who love even against what they believe God is and stands for. For God is love, and when you've loved beyond good sense, at personal current and cosmic risk, you are God's, and you *win*. You understand what love is. And you understand who God is, whether you realize or not, because you understand a level of love, most can't comprehend. No, you don't have to 'believe' in anything. You have to *love*.

Christ, in John 13 34-35, doesn't command us to believe. He commands us to love. Then we are His disciples. Then we are His children.

And I watched thousands of atypical fringe humans do exactly that, then return to their atypical lives as if their actions were never noticed or recorded. And if that's their other assumption, they'd be incorrect again.

If by chance you'd like further argument against the idea, common belief doesn't need re-evaluation simply because it is common belief:

"Why is it, as a culture we are more comfortable seeing two men holding guns than holding hands?" – Ernest Gaines

¹³ Therefore let us stop passing judgment on one another. Romans 14:13

² Each of us should please our neighbors for their good, to build them up. ³ For even Christ did not please himself but, as it is written: "The insults of those who insult you have fallen on me." Romans 15: 2-3

Hate misaligns our immortal and mortal being. –

Why are so many so quick to hate and exclude others?

The answer lies in what has become an inherent human characteristic based on our original method of receiving knowledge: Modeling/Apprenticing …*the tacit learning process*. Modeling is a more extensive way of describing imitation. People imitate others. It's based on a learned survival instinct and evolutionary in scope.

Humans try to imitate those they love and respect. This mainly starts when they're too young to realize they're physically finite beings. They also don't understand those who love them and mentor them are also imperfect physically finite beings, which isn't fully understood by those being emulated, which is again, a natural human flaw perpetuating our humanity.

People try to imitate those they feel are exhibiting admirable traits they wish to possess. This doesn't necessarily mean the traits they admire have anything to do with traits which are actually admirable. It is more congruent to the love, admiration, or proximity to the modeled human than it is a level of immortal right or wrong. And this is why we can teach our children to adopt what is wrong, so easily.

Modeling has been a strong human inclination for as long as humans have existed. It is the original way humans perpetuated their survival knowledge, and for millennia, the only way humans shared knowledge.

The process with which we passed information and skills to others, is called tacit learning (apprenticing). Humans spent the first 99.9 percent of our existence, apprenticing in order to receive the information and skills necessary to sustain existence. Only after the advent of mass-produced books, has this tacit learning process been altered. And with this eons-old practice, came the evolutionary instinct and instinctive human trait of modeling others.

The psychological term: *Modeling*:

Modeling comes in different degrees. One can purposefully imitate another's actions, demeanor, or beliefs, or one can do so without conscious effort, which is far more common and far less understood.

Children model their parents, guardians, and elders, whether conscious of their actions or not; whether agreeing they do, or not.

And the habits, beliefs, and demeanors adopted are far more extensive than humans realize. If humans realized the extent, maybe those being imitated would behave more responsibly.

Our children are not only watching …they're recording.

Conscious modeling is well understood and not the focus here. I would like to discuss how unconscious modeling affects humans.

Actions are what humans emulate, and actions are in fact, so strong, the modeled being's words are almost completely ignored when they don't correlate positively with their actions. Your actions are so deafening, those you model for can't hear a word you're saying.

Proof of unconscious modeling is best described by example:

HEADLINE: Children whose parents smoke are twice as likely to begin smoking between ages 13 and 32 as offspring of non-smokers.

http://www.washington.edu/news/2005/09/28/children-whose-parents-smoked-are-twice-as-likely-to-begin-smoking-between-ages-13-and-21-as-offspring-of-nonsmokers/

https://www.mailman.columbia.edu/public-health-now/news/if-mom-or-dad-smoker-their-teenager-more-likely-be-smoker-too

And this instinctive behavior isn't limited to human models. Humans are also modeling God, as currently / dogmatically understood. And not what we hear are God's words, but the well understood stories of God's supposed *actions*.

If God's words and actions aren't synchronous, then actions supersede words.

The Bible starts with perpetual human damnation for the bite of a fruit, then tells stories of God's firstborn human children (Israelites) being continuously conquered and enslaved due to their impurity and indiscretions. Why is no one questioning why God allowed barbarians with far more supposed impurity and far less godliness, to enslave them? There is enough incongruence for another book.

The old testament representation of God's *actions* show He's constantly disappointed if not disgusted, quick to anger, to punish, quick to hate, quick to condemn even those who would like to be His children. Righteous to the point of untenable, insistent, loving only as a reward; unloving otherwise. Almost impossible to please. He's vindictive and petty. Made laws that are impossible to uphold. Intolerant.

And humans are imitating their Father God, rather impressively. The more religious, the more the imitation. The more religious, the more intolerant. The more religious, the more demanding and unforgiving. God's words mean almost nothing and

His actions have been well documented, often repeated, and well recorded. Is God smoking a cigarette while telling His human children not to smoke?

Wrath: There are *still* people claiming, current natural calamities are the wrath of God. Two television stars just declared the latest two hurricanes, the wrath of God. Do you know the positive correlation between wisdom/intelligence and entertainment stardom? When you find a positive correlation, please share it.

Can you see why I had a problem with God that night? Can you see why God didn't have a problem with me having a problem?

Where did we get this fucked up idea of who God is?

Most of the examples are in our religious books. I'm going to focus on those in the Bible since I know it well enough to quote from it. The rest are in the religious interpretation of the Bible. Yes, the interpretation is often the culprit. More often than one would assume, the interpretation changes for religious convenience. Details are included.

EG: Sodom and Gomorrah / 1 Corinthians 6:9

Since almost all our assumptions who God is, come from the Bible, I'd like to first address the origins and foundation of the Bible, the people who supposedly wrote it, the people who actually wrote it, and their supposed ability to transcend the time and place of their existence.

Many far more famous and influential may disagree with my argument and conclusions. Many may redouble their efforts to convince others, the original premises believed without verification are still the truth. After all, it's what humans have believed for a very long time ...so it must be true. (See the struggle to change geocentric theory to heliocentric theory / creationism to evolution / any and all other false equivalencies believed for generations)

I'm not the first to perform or record this task. I'll just be another in the long line who will share this information, and I imagine humans will continue to share both perspectives until time passes on the humans teaching antiquated cult-like tribal ideas, or they begin to realize truth is tied to love because God is perfect, God is truth, and God is love.

What you can deduce from the *Love vs Hate* argument:

You can discern who is God's. Not by asking if they believe in God or Christ, but observing whether they love or hate.

Is the person *love*? Are they forgiving, empathetic, concerned with the plight of others ...or do they exclude, demean, oppress, *hate*?

# Chapter Five
## The Bible

There's a moment when you have to decide whether to stand up or be silent. – Malala Yousafzai

Why I'm about to write what I'm about to write:

For two thousand years, humans have waited for someone with religious authority (who knows God) to softly share the axiom, God is perfect …the real perfect. Not the human perfect. Not the perfect that has caused mayhem. Not the perfect that tortures God's children. Instead, the Perfect God showed me, and the child who went to heaven, and the doctor, and the countless others who have shared this exact experience and message.

Two thousand years and the soft, wonderful, loving, authoritative caress from a well-established religious organization, never came. Two thousand years we've waited, and everyone with the adulation and authority who could have changed the world by gently touching our cheek and telling us we're loved perfectly …never appeared.

I want to touch your cheek with the back of my hand, and softly whisper to you, you're loved beyond your wildest imagination and your God is *Perfect*! ...but I have no ability to be heard if I whisper. I have no influence. I'm nobody. Currently, there are regular instances where someone without notoriety shares the experience that they have encountered God and She is magnificent perfect love ...and the message is cheered, then forgotten as quickly as it's shared.

Those without fame get heard for a fleeting second ...or less.

...Unless someone punches a monster in the mouth.

Would I rather share my message with the soft touch of the back of my hand? Like God touched me as softly as He did, I want nothing more, as we wait for someone with prestige to tell us what I've told you ...what the young person told you ...what the esteemed doctor told you. –You are loved and protected beyond your wildest imagination. You really are. I swear. This message is very real and accurate.

But in order for the world to hear the message of an insignificant nobody, that nobody needs a message that gets the attention of entities the size and power of mythical creatures. And I've asked God: Father, how does this message get heard? I have no clout. I have no pulpit. I am nobody.

The pulpit people are sharing a different message, and I think my message is ...from God ...about love. The unconditional love of a perfect God. Not just for a few, but for everyone …with significant proof.

And God let me see the things that follow, under the premise, certain groups are not hearing the softly whispered message, so it's time to increase the message volume until the dragon-like entity notices and acknowledges the message.

So I'm about to punch a monster in the mouth, to get its attention, because the monster has been hurting some of you. And that isn't acceptable.

"Do not believe in anything simply because you have heard it. Do not believe in anything simply because it is spoken and rumored by many. Do not believe in anything simply because it is found written in your religious books. Do not believe in anything merely on the authority of your teachers and elders. Do not believe in traditions because they have been handed down for many generations. But after observation and analysis, when you find that anything agrees with reason and is conducive to the good and benefit of one and all, then accept it and live up to it." – Siddhartha Gautama

Many think the above quote is a fake quote. I personally have no idea what that means, but of course people have proclaimed it fake. Then they don't have to contemplate or digest its meaning.

Because if they evaluate the words, they might have to admit the content is sound and then they might realize they should adhere to it, and that would mean…well, you see the long slippery slope.

Personally, I don't care who wrote it or who is credited for saying it. I have a habit of measuring words, and can't for the life of me, find anything wrong …anything not pure …not enlightening, in that paragraph. In fact, I find the paragraph so profound, I try to model my intellectual life after it.

A history professor once taught me to measure the proclivity of everything I read. Is there an ulterior motive for someone's perspective? What does the author stand to gain from the words she or he has written? Measure their proximity to the information. Were they a first-hand witness? Were they told the events by a witness? Is the information hearsay? How many parties removed is the author from the information? How did the author verify the information?

I can't seem to find a proclivity in that paragraph. It seems pure, so I don't quite care who wrote it or when it was written. And if the translation precludes it from authenticity, then we have opened an entirely new can of worms, with regard to the Bible.

The book I'm about to re-evaluate hasn't met the same level of scrutiny as that quote. If you're personally offended by that sentence, please re-evaluate why. With re-evaluation, you may find the sentence isn't offensive.

The argument why the statement isn't offensive:

"Test all things and hold to that which is good." - Apostle Paul / 1 Thessalonians 5: 21

The Apostle Paul gives permission to question the wisdom and validity of the Bible, and for the harm and hate certain documents inside the Bible have caused and continue to cause ...I will.

ORIGINS OF THE BIBLE

The assumption: The Bible stories are legitimate and transcendent because they are included.

Why are we expected to base our primary spiritual perspective, on that assumption?

The assumption's primary argument: The people of those bible-creating councils measured transcendent meaning for inclusion.

These were people who didn't know where the sun went at night. People who didn't know the earth wasn't the center of the heavens and didn't know 'the heavens' included galaxies. For parts of the Old Testament: Bronze Age intellectuals.

Contemplate that for a moment.

The Bible, as a book, was commissioned in 325 CE by Emperor Constantine during the Council of Nicaea, and the first drafts were presented around 336 CE – more than 300 years after Christ's death. Since, its canonization (religious completion), it has been reworked countless times, by the organization charged with its preservation.

The governing organization had unfettered control over all aspects of the content. Whether or not they manipulated the content maliciously, has no bearing on this book's discussion. Historians and linguists have proven some Bible documents have been manipulated. Four such innocent possibilities are: inaccurate duplication, interpretation, translation, and modernization.

Think about the idea, through the turmoil of the dark-ages, with unregulated and unrestricted control over content and distribution, by an organization headed by some so ungodly, they are declared the ten small (evil) kings as supposedly referenced in Revelations – the Bible remained unscathed and pristine. What are the odds?

Now think about the idea, the book's founding documents come from a time and place well known for its less than advanced universal, cultural, and social beliefs. The society founding the book thought angels raised the sun each day and had no idea where the angels stored it at night. That is not meant to disparage. It is fact.

Then contemplate the current idea: Those teaching from the book believe God wrote the book, or the authors were divinely inspired, and every axiom inside should not be questioned.

The following is Bible content that does not project a fourteen billion year (minimum) old, wise, perfect Being who creates universes for fun. Please evaluate the following content so you can also measure that statement.

The first five Bible books – The Books of *Wisdom*:

Genesis has two conflicting creation stories. One follows the other. (Gen 1 & Gen 2) Linguists have proven they were written by at least two different authors and many believe, by two groups of authors. A story of Adam and Eve can be found in Zoroastrianism, which is also middle-eastern and precedes Judaism. The story of Noah is a plagiarism from The Epic of Gilgamesh, King of Uruk (stone tablet 11). Psalm 104 is a plagiarism of The Song of (Egypt Pharaoh) Akhenaten. The creation order of the above documents has been and is - easily verified.

Many religious believe Moses wrote the first 5 books in the Bible. But he couldn't have written Deuteronomy 34: 5 - 10 which describes his death.

My personal favorite excerpt, excluding the advice on how to treat your slaves, and who to stone to death without trial is: 2 Kings 2:23-24   The story of God sending two bears to maul forty-two teenagers to death, for calling Elisha 'baldy'. (The passage is enclosed.)

Archaic writings created by or credited to a two thousand year old middle-eastern culture, unaware of all modern human knowledge, with time inaccuracies, adopted stories handed down orally by pre-written-language societies crossing undefined and nebulous borders, retold in foreign languages, first written by scribes with suspect understanding, well after actual events, with questionable instruction, under edicts from unworldly, unmodern, spiritually questionable leaders, reinterpreted without pause through some of the most backward times in human history, for two-thousand years ...and people are adopting its edicts unevaluated.

Has anything else come from the middle-east over the last two thousand years that anyone wants to adopt unevaluated?

Who wrote each Bible document, is not open for discussion at this point. A discussion on that information is below and the information is also readily available but holds no bearing on this current discussion. This book will remain focused on the parameters already established, measuring only bible content for validity.

Many would like us to believe God wrote the Bible, or the Bible is God's direct word.
He condones slavery?
Deuteronomy 15:12-15; Ephesians 6:9; Colossians 4:1

He condones stoning someone to death for not being a virgin upon marriage?

Deuteronomy 22:13-21; Deuteronomy 22:22

...Mauling forty teenagers for calling someone 'baldy'?

Do they sound like the edicts and acts of a perfect God

...or...

...are they just stories of and from an ancient culture, which have been given more acclaim than originally requested or intended?

How much of the Bible did God write?

Ten lines? God wrote ten commandments, correct? But I've already proven there's an eleventh commandment: John 13: 34-35. In fact, that's the only commandment to come from the Being religion declares God from God, Light from Light, begotten, not made of one being with the Father. Christ and God the Father are compared later also.

The ten commandments are found in Exodus 20: 1-17. Moses is its believed author. Yet starting at Exodus 20: 24 and continuing through Exodus 21 – there are roughly forty additional commandments for humans and ten for oxen. God thinks highly of oxen. He took the time to share an additional ten commandments about them.

He doesn't take kindly to thieves. Exodus 22 has additional commandments for thieves which include selling them as slaves if they can't make restitution for what they've stolen. Exodus 22: 16 is a commandment. So is Exodus 22: 19, 21 and 22. Exodus 22: 23-24 states for the umpteenth time how God will kill those who break many of these additional commandments. Exodus 22: 25 – 31 also reads like commandments, as does Exodus 23: 1-19. Exodus 23: 20-33 explain quite clearly exactly how angry and unforgiving God is, with an additional commandment or two thrown in for good measure.

  To be honest, I lost count of the additional commandments at around fifty. How is it we consider only ten the official number? Weren't they all on tablets, or did God dictate the additional ones at a different time? They read as if they're all linked together. How did the ten become separate? The others follow in direct line without demarcation and are written quite clearly as if also directly from God. Who created the first ten demarcation? When and where was it divided?

  Is the reason these remaining commandments aren't given the same honor as the original ten, because they're acknowledged as pertaining to the specific time and place of their creation and not time-transcendent? We no longer own oxen. Yet the ten we hold sacred weren't time and place specific? God offers no demarcation, nor does Moses.

## MOSES

Moses supposedly lived roughly BCE 1400
Written language during the time of Moses

[Referenced work:]

[    Lester L. Grabbe says in *Ancient Israel*, page 117 that there were no pre-eighth century alphabetic writings in the area of Israel and Judah, except for the Gezer calendar which was probably Canaanite, early Hebrew and Canaanite writings being very difficult to distinguish

Exodus 24:4  And Moses wrote all the words of the Lord

Exodus 24:7 And he took the book of the covenant, and read in the audience of the people

### What language did Moses speak? Where was he from?

A cultural anthropologist and religious scholar who specializes in linguistics believes "it was unlikely Hebrew, as that is basically the language of the Canaanites around who the Hebrews eventually settled, and probably was adopted later. It likely would have been the dialect of the Medes, of whom his wife was a member and his father in law a priest (and he himself lived for years after he fled). Moses received the revelation in Eastern Canaan or Nabatea (most likely according to scholarly research) but in the country of the Kenites, who were Median by ethnicity. His revelation was accepted amongst those people, and many of them apparently joined the Hebrew people in their Exodus. This is the likely ancestor to modern Iranian languages, and even Avestan, and is an early form of Indo-Aryan languages, related to modern Persian and most Indian languages.

However, at some point, and probably within the next few generations, an oral tradition gave way to a translation in the Canaanite tongue, which eventually became what we now know as "the Holy Tongue", the Hebrew language, in a Proto-Hebrew dialect. It's the most logical answer and would be supported by linguistic scholarship.

However, I personally think the revelations were originally written in Hebrew, and ascribed to him later. None of the writings are in the first person, and they even describe his death. But many would disagree on that point, even though (as mentioned before) Deuteronomy 34:5-10 describes Moses's death.

Others believe phonetically written language may have started as early as BCE 1800 but many declare it would not have been Hebrew, but a combination of rough hieroglyphic pictures and symbols.

Egyptians also kept good societal records, yet show no records of Jews ever being slaves in Egypt. This is also confirmed by Israeli archeologists. Many archeologists and Egyptologists dispute the historical accuracy of the Exodus, but whether it is historically accurate or not, we cannot prove its authenticity or the exact time of Moses's existence. Some believe he lived around BCE 1275 (the recorded time of the Pharaoh's accomplishments), and the majority of linguists believe written language did not exist for another 200 years minimum. (recent findings of an Ostracon dated around BCE 1050)

Yet we have proof of written language from far before this time: The ***Epic of Gilgamesh*** is an epic poem from ancient Mesopotamia that is often regarded as the earliest surviving great work of literature. The literary history of Gilgamesh begins with five Sumerian poems about Bilgamesh (Sumerian for "Gilgamesh"), King of Uruk, dating from the Third Dynasty of Ur (c. 2100 BC).

That fact offers argument for written language during Moses's time, but also brings into question, the claim of the originality of the story of the Noah's Ark, which is estimated to have happened roughly BCE 2300 but with no written account until the creation of the Genesis scrolls, believed to be circa 6th or 5th century BCE.

Almost every ancient culture around the world has this epic flood story in its recorded history, which means these other cultures not only had flood survivors as well, but the story behind the event becomes more suspect.     ] [end referenced work]

### Other curious Bible author claims

I did an internet search on who wrote the Bible:

https://www.google.com/search?q=who+wrote+the+bible%3F&ie=utf-8&oe=utf-8

https://www.gotquestions.org/who-wrote-the-Bible.html

[ '… "According to 2 Timothy 3:16, Scripture is "breathed out" by God. Throughout the Bible, it is obvious that God is being quoted: over 400 times in the Bible, we find the words "thus says the Lord" (NKJV). The Bible refers to itself as the Word of God dozens of times (e.g., Psalm 119; Proverbs 30:5; Isaiah 40:8; 55:11; Jeremiah 23:29; John 17:17; Romans 10:17; Ephesians 6:17; Hebrews 4:12). The Bible is said to proceed from the mouth of God (Deuteronomy 8:3; Matthew 4:4)." …

"However, saying that God wrote the Bible does not mean He took pen in hand, grabbed some parchment, and physically wrote the text of Scripture. His "writing" of Scripture was not a physical action on His part. Rather, God's authorship was accomplished through the process of inspiration, as human writers wrote God's message.
So, it is also accurate to say that inspired men of God wrote the Bible." …'

'… "Only through divine inspiration could the Bible have been written so long ago, and over such a long period of time, and still be free of error and contradiction." …' ]

The Argument

**Warning**: You recognize where the theme of this book is leading. If you're uncomfortable with ideas that differ from our current typical accepted paradigms …if you choose to accept certain things unquestioningly, know the next segment and many sections of the rest of the book may fall between uncomfortable and uncomfortably paradigm adjusting.

If you need to die, not having contemplated a more thorough verification of truth regarding the accuracy of your religion, by all means, do so. You will be no worse for wear, as the perfect primary rules of the Perfect Being state. But understand we are here to learn.

Know also, you can do so at your own pace. God and you have all the time in existence …literally. But please, if you wish to stop here …please consider a deeper understanding of the definition of perfect, as it pertains to your God and the things He created. End your hatred, unacceptance, and exclusion in God's name, as you close this book and dismiss its secondary messages.

The premise of Adam and Eve or Free Will

6 Day Creation or 14 billion year ongoing event

>Spin: 6 'periods of time' wipes out the need to keep holy the 7th <u>DAY</u>.

2nd Creation timeline in Gen 2 or the original in Gen 1

Noah's Flood or The Epic of Gilgamesh

Pharaoh Akhenaten or Abraham as the 1st to acknowledge a single all-powerful God

**God vs The Bible**

The Bible Creation Story:

Is there a chance God doesn't remember the correct information or didn't quite relay the information correctly? Did the humans misinterpret the message, misunderstand the message, plagiarize the message or make the stories up, to fit their agenda at that time?

"*Thus says the Lord*" really doesn't take much effort to write, even if you're doing it on papyrus with a quill or stylus. What are the odds the quote was used once or twice in the Bible, inaccurately?

The Earth wasn't created in six days. God didn't condemn humans in perpetuity because someone bit a piece of fruit, and why did Cain build a city? He, his wife, son, mother, and father were the Earth's only inhabitants. And where did his wife come from?

God didn't flood the earth because He was disgusted with our impurity. The Adam and Eve, and Noah and flood stories are plagiarisms, and the six-day creation is a fourteen billion year ongoing event.

http://www.huffingtonpost.com/bart-d-ehrman/the-bible-telling-lies-to_b_840301.html

[ ... "Apart from the most rabid fundamentalists among us, nearly everyone admits the Bible might contain errors — a faulty creation story here, a historical mistake there, a contradiction or two in some other place. But is it possible that the problem is worse than that — that the Bible actually contains lies?

Most people wouldn't put it that way, since the Bible is, after all, sacred Scripture for millions on our planet. But good Christian scholars of the Bible, including the top Protestant and Catholic scholars of America, will tell you that the Bible is full of lies, even if they refuse to use the term. And here is the truth: Many of the books of the New Testament were written by people who lied about their identity, claiming to be a famous apostle — Peter, Paul or James — knowing full well they were someone else. In modern parlance, that is a lie, and a book written by someone who lies about his identity is a forgery" … ]

https://hwarmstrong.com/who-wrote-bible.htm

[ … "Some scholars say so many revisions occurred in the 100 years following Jesus' death that no one can be absolutely sure of the accuracy or authenticity of the Gospels, especially of the words the authors attributed to Jesus himself. "In over 40 years of oral transmission, the sayings of Jesus often were paraphrased," asserts Lane McGaughy, professor of religion at Willamette University in Salem, Oregon. … '

' … "Once written, many experts believe, The Gospels were redacted, or edited, repeatedly as they were copied and circulated among church elders during the late first and early 2nd Centuries." …'

' … "many modern scholars place the composition of Matthew quite late, between AD 80 and 100, making it implausible to some that Matthew the tax collector, one of Jesus' original 12 disciples, was really the writer". …'

' …a "majority of scholars deny that Luke 'the beloved physician' was the author" of Luke-Acts because he seems to commit historical errors that a companion of Paul could not have committed". … ]

I believe the people who wrote the bible could have believed they were ordained to do so and still have had difficulty due to influences of their time and place of existence, because as I write this, feeling like I'm compelled to – I continually remove my personal agenda from my narrative, to make sure my message stays on course – and I can't believe how hard it is. In fact, it's damn near impossible trying to write within objective perspectives and eliminating one's own opinion from the task.

Were the Bible authors sometimes strong enough to write parts purely? I believe so. Are there parts not written cleanly, or reworked, or meanings twisted through extensive retranslation (and human interpretation), until the message no longer serves God or His children? The proof is the multitude of attempted translations. Are there parts which no longer pertain to our time and place? Ten commandments about oxen, rules regarding how to treat your slaves, and who to stone to death, verify. Is our current version of the book completely pure, accurate, and without societal or human influence? No, for reasons just mentioned.

So once again, using me as my psychological sample, I'd say God inspires me to write this document and even helps me see perspectives not my own, but God doesn't force me to write, or give me orders to write specific words. I have free will to write what I wish and my personal baggage is great enough to find it difficult to keep out of the pile of things I'm sharing.

Back to the Bible...

Neither Paul nor Timothy wrote Timothy. It has references to the practices of a religious sect called the Gnostics who didn't exist until well after Paul's death, John may not have written significant parts of 'John'. Paul only wrote seven of the thirteen documents credited to him, and we can't figure out who wrote Hebrews, or Deuteronomy, for the reason stated above...and the list goes on.

And Moses might have written the first five books attributed to him, including Genesis, though the duplications in Genesis, called 'doublets', are so frequent, the document looks like it was written by two different groups and thrown together without concern for authenticity or redundancy. Remember, Deuteronomy describes his death.

But when measured against modern knowledge, the first five bible books read like the author had a time-limited intellectual perspective. It's safe to say the Genesis author(s) had no understanding how the universe was created, or how humans came to acquire their spiritual perspectives. The contradictions between the creation stories in Gen 1 and Gen 2 are a single page apart.

Scholars have substantive proof the Bible was assembled some three hundred years after Christ's death, by order of Emperor Constantine, and only God knows who revised the contents since records of revisions weren't kept. The organization holding unregulated control of the book's contents also experienced a rather 'ungodly', unrestricted, cult-like extended period, before reaching modern times. Yes, any organization that operates in secrecy is cult-like.

But I'm not concerned with author names, forgeries, or revisions. Like this document, my only concern is the content. If the words in the Bible represent a *perfect* God, I say we all declare those sections legitimate and worthy of adherence. If the words are anti-god and anti-human, I'm inclined to suggest the opposite.

Do we have to accept the book as a single entity? Absolutely not. It wasn't written or assembled as such. In fact, the opposite is true. Each document in the book was initially measured separately for inclusion and should be re-evaluated separately as well. Society has the ability and authority to evaluate individual passages for their messages, and eliminate ideas inconsistent with a perfect God, and the welfare of the human race.

Is there a precedent for such action? Merriam Webster did so in 1883. He removed all the sexual "filth not fit for humans to read", and called the reworked Bible "his greatest accomplishment".

The Book of Daniel – the prophecy of Daniel – has been proven inauthentic. The book was written during the time 'prophesized' and everything written about the time the prophet supposedly lived has been decertified. Was it always a lie? The secular world has no way of ever finding out, and only an organization with an ancient library could help.

The book of Timothy is invalidated by modern knowledge and an affront to the spiritual and physical definition of equality. Time always invalidates two-thousand-year-old social beliefs, no matter what sacred book houses them.

Leviticus looks like a five-year-old had a temper tantrum with a crayon, yet there are still preachers who like to take a single immature line and preach it as if the edict was directly from God, and ignore the rest of the laws accompanying that line, even though the Apostle Paul quotes a curse from Deuteronomy, in Galatians, warning those who do. (discussed later.)

Parts of Corinthians are brilliant and parts so misinterpreted, they have caused thousands of deaths.

The deaths of innocents are recorded, and discontinuation of this practice is being requested. If you cannot bother to authenticate the interpretation, and the interpretation causes human harm, especially death … please know, the words and your related actions are directly against your God. (Discussed in greater detail later)

The Bible authors may have tried their hardest to write what they believed. They may have even made conscious effort to transcend time, but the current bible is a perspective mainly pertaining to their specific biblical time and place, with bits and samples of true purity representing God sprinkled sporadically throughout its contents.

I do believe other parts of the Bible are unarguable. I love quoting the parts that speak of a perfect God, love, and forgiveness. Examples are throughout this book. But the opinion, the entire Bible is the direct word of God, and transcends time, is not fair to those who wrote it, preach it, read it, or wish to believe in it.

Some religious feel threatened by the backlash they perceive, against their hardline godly beliefs, and are re-trenching instead of re-evaluating, after noticing some are identifying excerpts incongruent with a wiser definition of spiritual perfection. The argument has been made, some two-thousand-year-old edicts from this book's specific earthly point of origin aren't as transcendent as some would like all to believe.

But those religious speaking loudest against this perceived threat seem to be the least informed regarding their beliefs. Many are being told, works like this book are Satanic and meant to do no more than spread doubt about their faith. Please separate faith and religion. Please understand it isn't necessary to separate faith and knowledge. Have faith in God. God exists and is perfect. Having faith in religion is not the same thing. That fact is argued extensively in Galatians.

If a belief goes against pure common sense, then maybe humans have changed and matured enough to have a new perspective on or knowledge of that story and its intended meaning …and then maybe a restructuring or reframing of that belief is in order. Even the unquestioning have adopted a new mindset regarding the six-day creation and have now reframed it to mean six 'periods of time'. Yes, some of us understand the six-period-of-time creation theory is actually a fourteen billion year ongoing event, but look how far some believers have come.

But the religious already acknowledge many of the invalid parts of the Bible.

Leviticus is a great example. In Leviticus, there are very few unrecognized invalid edicts. The religious themselves have already openly identified a good amount of the book's spiritual inaccuracies by ignoring the edicts stated, without a second thought.

The religious eat pork and shellfish. Religious males shave. Religious wear multi-fabric blend clothing. Many have tattoos. They no longer wear veils or adhere to the law against work on the Sabbath though religions have yet to decide what day the Sabbath is.

And but for one questionable Levitical law, the religious have unabashedly shown us Levitical law, as understood, is ignorable and less than wise or mature. All supposedly except one edict. One Levitical law is still held by some religious, as universal. It is mixed with the ignored laws. It isn't separate. It only holds one distinct difference to all the other invalid laws: It can be upheld by a majority of religious, with little effort, and can condemn others while those condemning believe (inaccurately) they can remain unaffected by their 'righteous condemnation'.

The law: The condemnation of homosexuality. The rest of the Levitical 'laws' have been discarded …and that one – right in the middle of all the other rejected decrees – stands. Even after the Apostle Paul stated concisely in Galatians 3:10:

All who rely on observing the law are **under a curse**, for it is written: "Cursed is everyone who does not continue to do *everything* written in the Book of the Law." - Gal 3:10

The quote in Gal 3:10 is twice - scripture. The enclosed quotation is Deuteronomy 27:26. Deuteronomy is a book of Law in the Bible. The Apostle Paul uses the Law to condemn all who adhere to any part of the law without obeying *every* part of the law. All who claim 'homosexuality is an abomination' are cursed.

One last Levitical law still needs to be recognized as childish trash, and then the entire book can be removed from our human future. Not to worry. The Vatican can lock a copy safely inside their secret vaulted library, for posterity. And people can go back to the intellectual concept: It isn't what goes in your mouth that makes you a good or bad person; it's what comes out of your mouth.

# Chapter Six
## Reframing Bible Stories

**Examining the Bible for Time Transcendence versus human time and place perspectives**

So, with the viewpoint that God wrote the book – as quoted from more than one (religiously affiliated) source which populated the internet search, when presented the question: 'Who wrote the Bible?' …let us delve into God's 'personality' as described by 'His own words'.

Internet search: 'God showing anger in the Bible'
[https://www.google.com/search?q=God+showing+anger+in+the+Bible&ie=utf-8&oe=utf-8_____ …populated…

First site:

'25 Bible verses about the anger of God, consequences'
https://bible.knowing-jesus.com/topics/Anger-Of-God,-Consequences

…Bible.knowing-Jesus.com

25 not so flattering descriptions of a not so loving god. ]

Second site:

[ Does God get angry? – (And the first five WORDS of the internet description:) 'Yes, **God** DOES get **angry**.'

https://www.gotquestions.org/does-God-get-angry.html

Website three declares it has provided the **TOP** 25 examples of God's anger from the Bible.

Website four tries to placate God's wrath as if wrath doesn't speak to us in simplistic terms.

Website seven: 'God's Furious Anger' ]

**Adam & Eve**

The more aware humans become, coupled with the unmeasurable increase of available information, the more things written two thousand years ago, begin to show inconsistencies.

In the first century, when Christianity was organized and its Bible assembled, there was no such thing as psychology. And even during the advent of psychology, religion remained irreproachable. Then incongruences started appearing in some otherwise unverified Christian beliefs:

A.   The idea, God planted a tree and forbade us from eating its fruit - directly contradicts two other basic human beliefs:

1. God is Perfect
2. Humans have free will.

**A Reframing** – without adjusting the incident whatsoever: Do you have free will?

If one believes humans have free will, how were we expected to discern right from wrong without knowing both right and wrong—good and evil? How could or why would an intelligent creature or being, expect that? Humans needed the knowledge of good and evil to decide between right and wrong – which means the entire premise: *Adam and Eve condemned all humankind by eating the fruit of the Tree of Knowledge* – which gave humans the knowledge of wrong and evil, cannot possibly be feasible because without knowing right from wrong / good from bad, humans would have no gauge how to enact their free will.

If you're inclined to adopt this new premise and agree that if there is an omnipotent perfect Being with a *minimum* age equaling the age of this universe, who loves and exists in perfection; making universes for living beings to enjoy, then allow me to present the Adam and Eve reframing…

What if God planted the beautiful tree with the tempting fruit in the middle of the garden *SO* humans would eat from it and learn the difference between right and wrong / good from evil? What if this is when we became sentient beings, and God's children? What if this is when we went from animals who knew nothing more than what a zebra or rabbit knows – to the higher life-forms we like to credit ourselves with being?

What if this coincided with an interpretation of us feeling like we were thrown out of a garden we weren't able to see as anything past how a rabbit or zebra sees it? The alternate perspective still fits the definition of, all of a sudden knowing we were naked. All of a sudden, we were *aware*.

Not all pre-modern human/apes partook, which is why our human lineage shows the split it shows: Apes and monkeys still exist. Their lineage didn't partake of the fruit.

My personal belief regarding the reframing of the antiquated story is: This is an example of just how unworldly and non-modern the original Bible authors were. And there are humans still teaching the original spiritual spin? Why? Would it have something to do with their wholehearted acceptance without engaging in rational intellectual process?

And why the average modern human doesn't run screaming from that spiritual monster when presented the original interpretation of who God is, can only be explained one way: Their inability to process the irrationality, the story depicts. I've tried identifying the reasons for this inability:

1. Age of indoctrination.
2. Spiritual maturity
3. A desire for a spiritual connection with promises of eternal well-being

4. The assumption there can't possibly be discrepancies in such long-believed religious paradigms

You aren't less human in any way for not being able to rationalize the events depicted. Almost all humans fit into multiple categories above. It is only when religion quells natural spiritual hopes and expectations, does one have a moment of pause regarding the promises that seem rational at first glance …or thirtieth glance, when you're instructed to just take certain assumptions on 'faith alone'.

My curiosity extends when I ask, faith in what? Religion? Religious edicts? …Or God! One entity tells me, ignore intellectual shortcomings and be satisfied with current knowledge, and the other tells me to evaluate everything and progress as a learning being – under the premise, God is the perfect teacher.

**The Ramifications of the Adam and Eve Story**: The idea, no perfect being would be so cruel as to plant a tree with the best fruit in the middle of the garden, and then tell His children not to eat it, leads to the notion, either the Being is perfect and did no such thing or the Being is flawed, and the story is accurate.

Reframing the Adam and Eve story leads to additional points of contention. If there was no perpetual offense of *original* sin, there is no need for equal perpetual reconciliation. Not to worry, believers. Christ is still everything you think and need Him to be. But if you're one of Christ's supposed disciples who has never personally read a word He uttered, how do you consider yourself one of His followers anyway? Two thousand years ago, they called Him *teacher*, for a reason. He shared some amazing knowledge. Read some and judge for yourself.

**Original Sin**

So why would such a preposterous story regarding a demon god and his extreme and irrational punishment perpetuate, when in fact, if this re-evaluated and reframed version was our paradigm, our view of God would more accurately represent the benevolent God we actually have? You know …the One who is 'Love' and 'Forgiveness'?

I can think of one overwhelming reason, and will not share. My logic places religion in a certain light. You're free to come to your own conclusion regarding the discrepancy.

Original Sin: You're doomed because you were born. You're doomed because your parents wanted a baby to love, and made you. You're born doomed …because God is love?

Reframing the Adam and Eve story wipes out the necessity of redemption for the 'original sin' we're taught we're *guilty* of, and consequently, the need to participate in and perform the religious rituals our religious organizations suggest, to save our eternal lives.

The reframed story also makes a good argument, Christ wasn't crucified for this reason. I'm not saying he was or wasn't, but without *original sin*, there is no need for the redeeming action. Think of the industry that would collapse if this spin was adopted. They'd have to resort to selling billion dollar paintings.

For those who wish to contemplate the ramifications…

The three scenarios regarding crucifixion:

Christ was crucified for our (original) sins.

Christ's crucifixion had nothing to do with original sin (or God).

Christ was not crucified.

Do any of these three scenarios affect Christ's proposed deity? If Christ was God before His human birth, would He lose His deity if not crucified? Does Christ not being crucified make Him less perfect or brilliant? There's no need to discredit Christ for any circumstance. His teachings on love and forgiveness are brilliant …Godlike. Christ was better at love/forgive than the bible-given stories of God the Creator.

The de-legitimization of original sin wipes out the need for the redeeming act, and the de-legitimization of the necessity for a redeeming act wipes out the need to believe in it. (What a scary snowball on an even more frighteningly slippery slope.)

No worries. The need to *believe* in order to be *saved* has already been modified and is discussed extensively in a bit, but remember, you already own heaven. Your God is *Perfect*.

The 6 Day Creation story

It is now so questioned, the religious have put a recovery spin on the Creation Story. They now profess, it was 6 'periods of time', which is fine as soon as they then associate their reframing with the need to keep holy the Sabbath because God rested on the $7^{th}$ 'period of time', which became the Sabbath. And if God rested on the $7^{th}$ 'period of time', does that mean we no longer have to go to church on the $7^{th}$ day – but instead, must show up on the $7^{th}$ 'period of time'?

Please ignore the fact that the $7^{th}$ day is Saturday, and Christ specifically spoke against praying in public, in His *Sermon on the Mount* (Matthew 5 – 7).

With examination, the religious story fails all modern intellectual scrutiny and must be deemed: false. Is it purposefully false? Absolutely not. Does that fact make it anything other than false?

Some will feel emotional outrage at these statements. If these statements are accurate, does there have to be an emotional connection?

### Noah

The second greatest example of God's supposed wrath is the Noah's Ark story. We'll ignore the argument, what did the Lions eat during the forty days, because when you read about the stone tablet displaying the Epic of Gilgamesh, King of Ur, and find out the entire Noah's Ark story is plagiarized, you won't have to worry about what the Lions ate.

Modern man views plagiarisms negatively, but we must understand the context and foundation of antiquated plagiarisms in order to understand the reasoning behind them.

These stories are far older than written language, and country borders were far less a concern for travelers and nation-states than they are now. Plagiarisms from that time are just shared stories, as nomads and travelers moved through regions. None of these stories were owned by the people sharing them. None of these stories were the property of any one ancient tribe.

To give them a tribe of origin is what social sciences call ethnocentrism ...and inaccurate. To give them time-transcendent validity, with no proof of validation is... (Please fill in your conclusion.)

The ancient plagiarisms don't have a negative context or foundation. Retelling stories was how information was shared during pre-writing cultures. But it was also how they passed their time, and a substantial part of their social entertainment. Accordingly, the stories held the variation of significance, stories today merit. Certain stories are news, whether local, regional or world-wide, others are entertainment, some are non-fiction, some are fiction.

But the most alarming aspect of the Noah's Ark plagiarism is the religious spin certain religions have placed on the story. We have proof the story is plagiarized, but the problem goes well beyond the plagiarism. Humans get their concept of God from the spin the Bible portrays. The Bible / Noah's Ark spin: God is this impossible to please, heartless unforgiving omnipotent ogre who is so completely displeased by our lives and actions, He needed to wipe us from the face of the earth.

Stories of the flood are found around the world, including *The Epic of Gilgamesh*, but the Noah's Ark Bible story is the only one with an ominous ogre-god spin.

Flood stories around the world prove people survived around the world, which means animals survived around the world, which is inconsistent with the specific Bible version of the story, making certain physical assumptions inaccurate, which makes the spiritual angles, inaccurate. And when one significant piece of a story is found incorrect, the remaining parts of the story must be considered less than truthful.

And when one story from these storytellers can be found incorrect, all like insights by the same authors are also questionable, and no more than a specific tribal spin based on the authors' inclinations and perceptions.

I'm not a fan of words like 'untruth' or 'alternative truth' – something not true is false, and something false, repeated fifty times with fifty different examples, is false.

The idea the story states, God is not only directly responsible for the event, but also, God kills everyone because He's disgusted with how 'impure' and 'contemptible' we are – is false – and based on primitive beliefs of a primitive and unworldly tribe of people, influenced by the myopic perceptions of their time and place of existence.

There is no compromise to this fact. Compromise to this fact has led us in wrong directions by misguided humans since religion's inception. God is perfect and there is no part of this story or any 'God the Destroyer' story that is accurate. God is perfect and perfect all-powerful Beings aren't also immature, continually and constantly displeased, unloving callous ogres. If your God has any of these qualities, run screaming from Him and into the arms of MY God. My God is Perfect love/forgiveness.

Or better yet: Realize YOUR God is perfect love and forgiveness and give up the two-thousand-year-old inaccuracies your religions have fed you and your ancestors for two-thousand years.

The erroneous Ark story's erroneous perception also makes any and all other preachings of any such anger, annoyance, irritation, vindictiveness, cruelty, maliciousness, fury, rage, wrath, and spitefulness – equally erroneous, (False / inaccurate / incorrect / deceitful) and it's time current humans realize it.

And humans do not advance as sentient beings until they recognize certain Bible excerpts are not written by God or anyone transcending time and place but instead are the perceptions of a small tribe of people, existing in a less-than-modern time and place. The errors and inaccuracies prove it. (I don't prove it. I am only stating what the inaccuracies prove)

A good example: Judges 19 (The rape, murder and dismemberment story): A story without specific facts, names, moral, or transcendent meaning. The book it is in is claimed to be 'first written', roughly 500 to 600 years before Christ; most likely from oral stories perpetuated due to their lack of any other form of news or entertainment …and some Bronze Age Scholars decided it should influence humans perpetually? Humans go one better: Some *current* religious scholars think it should influence humans perpetually. Their reason: Inclusion. It's in the bible, so it must have important transcendent meaning. (The assumption)

You can read the thirteen paragraph story, and see for yourself if the assumption is valid.

https://www.biblegateway.com/passage/?search=Judges+19&version=NIV

We accept things without evaluation or verification and it seems like a good time in the history of man, to acknowledge some Bible misconceptions. All things falling under the heading of unquestionable – need to be questioned. Nothing is unquestionable. God made our existence on the premise: We are here to learn. Question everything. We do not learn until we question. Nothing is beyond questioning, and the only beings we lie to when we do not honor that premise, is us.

And any organizations telling us, we must believe in things without question, are manipulating us and counting on us to be too busy, lazy, or unintelligent to call them out. Please don't allow your enemies to convince you to be against you. Please question everything, starting with anyone telling you not to question everything.

It can be argued, many who teach the idea, the Bible is God's direct words, have no interest in discovering the truth. They have their agenda; their righteous unfounded reasoning behind their proclivities, and their 'religious' argument.

Either they haven't read the book they profess as timeless truth and written by God, or they have read it and ignore many parts, including Matthew 5-7, The Sermon on the Mount, where Christ derides gathering in a building to publicly declare one's religious righteousness, then explains, we should pray in secret to a God who hears in secret, after forgiving others for any offense they've committed against us.

…Kinda sounds like my love/forgive discourse, doesn't it?

Why else would these preachers exclaim every Bible word 'sacred', then proceed to ignore so many of the 'sacred' words? How can *The Sermon on the Mount* be so blatantly ignored? (You can look it up, but it's included and discussed.)

**The Dogmatic Description of God**

Humans have come to understand the dogmatic description of God, whether a member of a religion or not. Stories of God have permeated our society and culture, but we don't listen to the words attributed to God. We listen to the words describing God's actions, as portrayed by middle-eastern tribesmen who lived two to three thousand years ago.

What people don't understand is, the stories recounting God's actions are from a perspective tainted by the time, place, and circumstances surrounding the authors' biblical-era existence. There is no such thing as 'transcending time'. Humans have 7.5 billion current living human examples of no one rising above or going beyond their current existence, and beyond speculation, humans have no recorded incident of any human doing so in the past. Here we are. Here we stay. No exceptions.

We perceive God through his human representation though, and like good children, are modeling that antiquated perception of Him as Father. Accordingly, we need to revisit who God is, and from what I can gather from my edict to share these experiences and perspectives, I'm under the impression, someone or something else is also wishing humans revisit their current perception of God.

This opinion is not necessarily new or previously unstated. I only hope to reintroduce discarded viewpoints, in the hope of helping others see a Being whose love and forgiveness are boundless, beyond the human scope, and currently being greatly misrepresented.

I have ideas why the misrepresentation has occurred, and it would be easy to over-generalize the reason: Human imperfection. But rarely do simple explanations suffice for complex issues, so I'll share a more in-depth explanation, though I realize I only see through my eyes.

Certain antiquated perspectives from religious guidebooks are being re-emphasized when they should have been invalidated by now, but those who control realize these sections are best used to manipulate others. Human manipulation is why certain excerpts were included in the Bible, and it could be argued, those in control are re-emphasizing those passages for their purpose, with little to no interest in God's purpose.

Dear religious, please refocus on God's originally intended messages of love and forgive, and stop spreading fear and hatred in the name of the unconditionally loving and perfectly forgiving God.

The religious have been dividing the bible between legitimate and non-legitimate sections, for as long as they've had it. It's time to acknowledge this practice and address the books' societal directives which no longer serve humans. We can then write a new Bible storyline using the information we've gained in the past two thousand years, and move our human narrative forward, never again perceiving a book as 'time transcendent'. No human work is time transcendent. Humans aren't capable. Our perspectives are influenced by our experiences.

Problem: If a rewrite of the Bible would ever be considered, the religious who would volunteer to write a revised perspective are undoubtedly unqualified, and thus disqualified to do so. They have an agenda that disqualifies them. They'll swear differently because they don't understand their failed perspective. They would have to be removed from their current paradigms and psychology proves that, impossible. They're the new five-year-olds with crayons ready. Any acceptance of any attempt on their part will fail the human race.

Certain passages of the Bible and Quran were wonderful for what they served. But those times have passed and it's time humans embrace the concepts of moving forward. We can if we want, discover and enjoy some amazing new things about our universe. We're about to break through some well-established physics self-limitations if we embrace our journey and stop being afraid to move forward.

I know many humans fear change, but we always seem to embrace our current time, when our current time is never what it was, even forty years prior. Time has proven…our history has proven, moving forward is far more pleasurable than attempting to stop our journey. Every aspect of religions' attempts at stopping the human journey have been distressing mistakes, and always historical embarrassments.

**Christ vs God the Creator**

I expect many to be confused, if not startled by the title of this next discussion. We've been led to believe God and Christ are one in the same Being, and the idea They're opposed in any way is confusing, if not startling.

…God from God. Light from Light. Begotten, not made. One Being with the Father. - This is the Christian creed.

Christ's relationship to God is not a concern for this specific discussion, but I think it's safe to say, Christ was and is different from the rest of mankind. His place in the spiritual hierarchy has no bearing on this discourse because this discussion is based solely on the results derived from measuring the actions and teachings currently attributed to the Christ, and whether or not they coincide with the actions we currently attribute to God the Father.

And when the two are measured side by side, a distinct difference appears. But the creed states, they are one Being. So either, the concept of them being one Being is incorrect, or the explanation and subsequent attributing actions of either God the Father or God the Son, are inaccurate.

You may be able to accept this disparity. I chose to search for reasons why this difference exists and found an argument supporting my previous theories stating God the Father is not what we currently believe, and the interpretation of God the Father is through the perspective of authors mired in their time and place of existence …and inaccurate.

The Christ spoke of and acted out, a love for friends *and* enemies. The Christ spoke of and acted out, forgiveness without measure or hesitation. The Father is described as angry, unforgiving, and cruel, even by those who preach He is perfect. The Christ is just the opposite, kind to a fault, loving to a fault, forgiving to a fault, gentle to a fault; sharing His own life force with supposedly completely 'unworthy' strangers.

One Being with the Father. God from God. Light from Light.

Believers believe the Son is the Father. Does anyone need an argument why believers should then also believe the Father is the Son?

2 Kings 2:23-24   Elisha Is Jeered

$^{23}$From there Elisha went up to Bethel. As he was walking along the road, some boys came out of the town and jeered at him. "Get out of here, baldy!" they said. "Get out of here, baldy!" $^{24}$He turned around, looked at them and called down a curse on them in the name of the Lord. Then two bears came out of the woods and mauled forty-two of the boys.

Love/forgive? Are there no flaws in the bible?

2 Kings 2:23-24 is an example of a depiction of cold heartless evil perpetrated by the Creator God, beyond all physical or spiritual justice, and Christ never raised a hand in anger, portrayed as meek, mild, and as loving as any creature ever existing – and told us repeatedly: LOVE/FORGIVE beyond all expectation – in order to be God's.

Is Christ the Son a renegade not emulating the Father, or are the Son and Father the same? For all the messages that say They are

'God from God'– the Bible would insist the Father and son are very different and the Father borders on a raging demon.

Which is it? Or who wrote the inaccuracies depicting the raving lunatic demon version of an unconditionally loving caring Father …and why?

PS: There isn't a single mention of a third separate Being of the holy trinity in the entire original old or new testament. The original concept of a Holy Spirit is God's invisible active force. The concept of the Holy Spirit as a separate being doesn't get presented or ratified until after the first century.

http://www.auburn.edu/~allenkc/trinity.html#_1_6

There are now many bible references to this third being, but none in the original Christian or Jewish beliefs. Matthew 28:19 quotes Jesus referencing the Holy Spirit as a separate entity, but the line may have been reworked. Eusebius, one of those originally commissioned to assemble the current bible, quotes the text: "…make disciples of the Gentiles in my name" …and not "in the name of the Father, the Son, and the holy ghost", as currently quoted.

Mr. Constantine (or Tertullian A.D. 145-220 / Cappadocians) had more input into the new religion than he (they) had intellectual license, but the new religion doesn't get legitimized without Constantine's blessing, so compromises were made. The concept of the holy spirit being a third separate deity is one such compromise.

Those ruling the fledgling version of Christianity wanted nothing more than Constantine's endorsement, based solely on his prestige, and many were willing to sacrifice some accuracy for the testimonial. Not to mention, those who weren't willing didn't live long after their dissent.

He also decided Christ's official birth date …and missed. He had his reasons for picking the day he picked, with no concern for the actual date. He also decided Christians should worship on Sunday, which was the day the pagans worshiped the Sun god and the 1$^{st}$ day of the week. The Sabbath is supposed to be the 7$^{th}$ day, which is Saturday.

If any are thinking, Constantine was divinely inspired, please note: He boiled his wife, alive, and murdered his oldest son, *after* converting to Christianity.   Not godly. Just powerful.

# Chapter Seven
## Earning Heaven

You can do nothing to earn heaven.

⁸ For it is by grace you have been saved, through faith—and this is not from yourselves, it is the gift of God— ⁹ not by works, so that no one can boast. **Ephesians 2: 8-9 (Author: Apostle Paul)**

Yes, you've heard the message before. Yes, it's the Christian message. Yes, Christians twisted the message to say, there's nothing you can do to earn heaven, *except believe in Christ.*

All who preach the Christian faith say: "There is nothing you can do to earn heaven. All you have to do is believe." I believe Christ said the first sentence. "There is nothing you can do to earn heaven."

I believe religion added, "All you have to do is believe in God."

The extended argument…

https://www.gotquestions.org/contribute-salvation.html

[    Q: Do we contribute anything to our own salvation?
A: No …

"As it is written, there is none righteous, no, not one." Romans 3:10    ]

Take a moment to study the biblically based reply. Do religious organizations infer that sentence to mean, by birthright, all humans are not righteous enough to gain heaven, and unless you adhere to certain requisites, your salvation is in jeopardy? Only through 'our religion' can you find redemption, and for a weekly obligation, we'll help you gain salvation. Oh, please understand you'll never be cured. You not only have to adhere to our edicts through life, but there will also be an exit fee because we give final approval before you're on your way to your final resting place.

Back to the website – QUOTED:

[ 'First, from a practical point of view, let's assume that a person does contribute something to his salvation. If that were possible, who would get the credit in heaven? If man somehow contributes to his own salvation, it would follow that man himself gets the credit. And if man gets the credit, this certainly will detract from God's getting the credit. If it were possible to contribute something to attain heaven, then each person upon his arrival would be patting himself on the back because of what he did in order to obtain heavenly citizenship. These same people would be singing, "Praise myself, I contributed to my own salvation." It is unthinkable that people in heaven will be worshiping self rather than God. God said, "I will not give my glory to another" (Isaiah 42:8; 42:11).'

'From a biblical point of view, mankind contributes nothing at all to his salvation. The problem with humanity is their sinfulness. Theologians normally refer to this as "total depravity." Total depravity is the belief that mankind is sinful throughout and can do nothing of himself to earn God's favor. Because of this sinful state, mankind wants nothing to do with God (see especially Romans 1:18-32). It is safe to say that because mankind is totally depraved, mankind chooses to sin, loves to sin, defends sin, and glories in sin.'

Because of man's sinful predicament, he is in need of God's direct intervention. This intervention has been provided by Jesus Christ, the mediator between sinful humanity and righteous God (1 Timothy 2:5). As already stated, mankind wants nothing to do with God, but God wants everything to do with man. This is why He sent his son Jesus Christ to die for the sins of humanity—God's perfect substitution (1 Timothy 2:6). Because Jesus died, through faith mankind can be declared justified, declared righteous (Romans 5:1). By faith, the person is redeemed, bought out of the slave market of sin, and set free from it (1 Peter 1:18-19).

These acts just mentioned—substitution, justification, redemption—are just a few that are provided for completely by God, and devoid completely of anything human. The Bible is clear that mankind cannot contribute anything to his salvation. Any time someone thinks he can contribute, he is, in essence, working for his salvation, which is clearly against the Bible's statements (see Ephesians 2:8-9). Even faith itself is a gift from God. Salvation is a free gift from God (Romans 6:23), and since it is a gift, there is nothing you can do to earn it. All you have to do is take the gift.

"But to all who have received him (i.e., Jesus)—those who believe in his name—he has given the right to become God's children" (John 1:12).' ]

(…total depravity / man's predicament by birthright…)

**Resource:** Faith Alone: The Evangelical Doctrine of Justification by R.C. Sproul

[ "BY FAITH ALONE !" It is shouted repeatedly. "BY FAITH ALONE !"

"That if thou shalt confess with thy mouth the Lord Jesus, and shalt believe in thine heart that God has raised him from the dead, thou shalt be saved." Romans 10: 9-10, 13   ]

> But *believing* is a conscious act, so if 'believing' earns you heaven, you could boast, you've earned heaven
> *…and there's nothing you can do to earn heaven.*

News to all non-psychology majors: 'BELIEVING' in something (FAITH) is a conscious act. You, by believing Christ is God...are DOING SOMETHING consciously to earn heaven. You can 'believe' and be saved or 'not believe' and not be saved. – Conscious act.

You can profess and be saved or not profess and not be saved. – Conscious act.

No matter how you twist it, faith is a conscious choice. You're doing something to earn heaven. But the Bible says you can't do anything to gain heaven. You just read how many pages of Bible quotes and religious explanation?

Christ said the same thing, but not the way the two-thousand-year-old human authors or their medieval counterparts perceived or projected.

One of the many shortcomings of pre-modern thinking is the inability of pre-modern man to understand the psychology of human thought. Pre-modern humans didn't study the human mind. Pre-modern humans didn't give a thought to human thought, and that shortcoming offers insight into all failed attempts to transcend time, especially on a religious basis.

And there is no more glaring example of this than the idea, nothing can be done to earn heaven ...except *believe* God is the savior. And as soon as that is the requisite, there is a problem with the premise: You can't earn heaven. It's a problem pre-modern man couldn't fathom, and one that is glaringly obvious to anyone studying psychology.

*Believing* is something someone chooses to do and contradicts the idea there's nothing you can do to earn heaven. Is there nothing …or do you have to believe? The idea, you *can't earn heaven* unless you *earn heaven* by believing, is psychologically discordant.

There is nothing you can do to earn heaven. GOD does it all. Actually, God already did it all. Like a human mother and father did everything necessary for their child to be their child for their entire physical life.

A practical way to understand the argument:

What does your child have to do to remain your child? Once you have a child, is there any way that child doesn't remain your child during their entire existence? Does the child need to acknowledge she or he is yours? Do they have to visit you weekly? Do they have to be 'good'? How about visit a relative weekly, so the relative can report attendance? Does the child have to think a certain way? Adhere to certain societal beliefs?

Like your child, who has to do nothing to remain your child, so you also have to do nothing to remain God's child …and this isn't my edict, nor did I make this idea up for this book. It is the founding basis of Christ's and the Christian religion's message.

You cannot earn heaven.

That was the Christian message two thousand years ago that a few more than a few organizations seem to have manipulated over the years for their personal and organizational gain, but holds true since God created children. We have to do nothing to remain God's children.

Our access ticket into the spiritual universe (heaven) is already purchased, just like those two thousand years ago believed …just like God said, and His word is a promise. God is perfect, and Her edict has been set as currently believed: We're God's children.

The deal is done, and you …like your child …have to do nothing. What needs to be done has been done by the One who created you. You're good to go. A sentient being forever. God makes nothing sentient - temporary. She has no need.

Your dead loved-ones are also good. They're either alive and well in the spirit world, or back to living another existence on one of the 220,000 planets with intelligent life on it, in our universe …or possibly in another universe. But one way or the other, they're in good hands. Their Mother/Father is *Perfect*.

Your enemies are good too. Loved just like you. So consider dropping the petty differences and understand we're all related and equal.

Oh, and if you don't believe in God, or the idea God is God …you go to heaven. (Yes that will make some 'believers' unhappy.)

What did God say to the obedient son, after he complained the father gave the prodigal son an equal share? "Have I not given you everything I promised?"

Further explanation confirming Christ's meaning and refuting the Bible authors' spin: This also validates the argument: God is Perfect.

What does your (Earthly/Physical) child have to do to remain your child, once it is borne of you or declared yours legally and intentionally if purposefully adopted by you?

Nothing. No exit test. No requisite. No continual confirmation. No need for communion. Yours. And though we believe we're finite beings, we'd like to believe our children are ours through eternity if possible. The work has been done, and none of it by your child.

Why would you then think you can comprehend this concept without effort at your cosmic (immortal) age, and the eons old Perfect Being cannot? You choose beyond doubt or question to adhere to this edict, being a creature of moments of existence, and this great and perfect Being, who has supposedly existed for eons, with wisdom, knowledge, and power accordingly, doesn't have the ability or notion? Your existence here is finite and your cosmic knowledge cut off from past learning experiences, yet within miniscule earth years, you get the concept, and by chance, this eons-old perfect Being doesn't?

If He doesn't, does that mean God could learn from humans about loving a child? Or is God *perfect* at it, and we get our ideas about loving our children *from* Him. What seems more feasible?

We're God's children. Done deal. You have to do nothing. You can do nothing. You're His because *God* is Perfect. And She is Perfect because She chooses to be. Like we would choose if we had a choice.

All I did was re-evaluate religious paradigms and show you with scripture, you're guaranteed heaven – using quotes straight from The Bible.

Smile! You're good to go.

That's the message Christ shared while here. That message doesn't serve religion. It serves you — God's 'church'.

The <u>actual</u> definition of **Church**: God's children. The congregation. *We're* the 'congregation'. *Humans* are God's 'church'.

By believing: confessing 'Christ is God' is your ticket to heaven, you attempt to take control of your spiritual destiny. Sorry. We don't control our spiritual destiny. We're days old beings. Cosmic newborns. We as human parents don't give our newborns control over life decisions. Our eons-old Father doesn't give us control over our immortal life-decisions.

I know the concept of removing your eternal well-being from your control, sounds uncomfortable. It's like flying in an airplane. In order to be comfortable flying, you must understand you don't have control of your life for the duration of the flight. Those uncomfortable flying ...white-knuckle flyers... are just showing their inability to release control over a certain aspect of their life, for the allotted time of the flight. It's normal. It is human.

And the airplane pilot doesn't need your help flying. Can you see, the pilot knows you don't have the ability?

'But that isn't acceptable. We humans HAVE to do something, otherwise we lose control over our salvation. And the current nothing (Believing / Faith) is an easy something.'

No. Nothing you do can earn you heaven. Your ticket has been bought and paid for. You're in.

The opposing argument: being created under the terms we're almost all guaranteed to spend eternity in torment, is irrational. A loving God who by default, condemns all but a handful (144K) of those forced to enter this universe? And when that concept is truly accepted, who would dare create a child?

We're GOD's. Done deal. You and everyone you know and love are more alright and more loved than you could possibly ever comprehend. And we're brothers and sisters. One tribe.

None of these messages are new. We just haven't understood them correctly, for a lot of reasons, human and otherwise. Please see the simplicity and know that's a sign of God's perfection.

Christ shared a few other amazing facts that were omitted or misinterpreted, which will be shared. They're all great. God is great. An all-loving all-forgiving perfect Being who makes universes for fun and wants you to call Him 'dad'. He's Perfect!

An unexplained aspect of God's love

God loves His children unconditionally, and the greatest example is your infinite *spiritual protection*. Your immortal being has been mentioned countless times throughout human history. What hasn't been mentioned, due to religion's agenda is, you're spiritually *God protected*. Your spiritual being cannot be destroyed by any physical act occurring in the physical realm.

Besides love and forgiveness, this is your ultimate gift. You are not only God's, but God protects you like parents protect their children. The difference: God is the ultimate protector since all exists as God wishes.

God has no problem loving / forgiving, and has no need to be 'found'. Instead just loves you and watches you love, forgive, learn and experience all existence.

A quick backtrack to the inner-city 'Wall of Love' event: I mentioned, the group which ridiculed religion and the god religion supposedly represented, by loving against religion's and God's edict – pleased God by doing so. Not whether they find Him or not. Whether they LOVE or not. They're no less God's children than those who spend half their waking week in church. In fact, they're the people God is teaching at the moment. They're the ones He's bothering with. God is giving them life situations, almost unbearable at times, sometimes life-threatening, though we can't be destroyed spiritually (our true being).

Certain people do not, and most likely will not understand, but God is forging them; teaching them about love, so they someday, after countless more lessons, know love so completely, they become the spiritual beings God wishes they become. But this creation takes time and many lessons. And today, God will teach some, and in order to do that, some will remain untaught at the moment, running around like uncontrolled newborns. No worries, they get taught too. All of us do.

But does God care whether you find Him? It has no bearing on God or you and counts for what it looks like it counts for – nothing.

And sitting in church no more makes you God's child, than sitting in a garage makes you a car. (not original, but so true)

Instead, show love and acceptance / brotherhood and caring, and it will equal a lifetime sitting in church, though the pastor will argue otherwise. She or He can't buy groceries unless they convince you otherwise and she or he likes to eat, which nullifies their dissenting argument.

Coincidentally, I just freed up your Sundays, but let me offer additional proof. I wouldn't want you to be unsure. I now bring a (very old) new light to the whole Sunday church premise using Christ's words in the Bible.

Make your counter-argument, dear preachers.

It's okay. Christ admonished church-goers first, in the Sermon on the Mount, when He taught us how to pray: Matthew 6: 5-8

[5]And when you pray, do not be like the hypocrites, for they love to pray standing in the synagogues (what churches were called at that time) and on the street corners to be seen by others. Truly I tell you, they have received their reward in full. [6] But when you pray, go into your room, close the door and pray to your Father, who is unseen. Then your Father, who sees what is done in secret, will reward you. [7] And when you pray, do not keep on babbling like pagans, for they think they will be heard because of their many words. [8] Do not be like them, for your Father knows what you need before you ask him.

Of course, you're more than welcome to spend time in a church. You may spend time anywhere you see fit as long as it harms no one.

My contention is with the religions and preachers who preach righteous hate and exclusion …who condemn some of God's children, such as LGBT, as if a billions-year-old perfect God makes mistakes, humans can identify.

Please also *reconsider* the idea, being a good Christian involves denying others the basic inalienable human rights the majority have and insist on. It is the opposite of God's message. It is the opposite of human decency. It opposes what Christ taught.

But you can still give the mega pastor and or television pastor money, or you can choose to find a source that would benefit the poor, which is one of the God-representing Bible suggestions. (See: Matthew 6: 1-4)

If this all seems too simple to be true, understand it is. Humans add burdens. God removes burdens (He called them yokes). Humans make the simple complicated. God takes the complicated and makes it simple. When you see that being done, maybe God's hand is in it.

[11] When I was a child, I talked like a child, I thought like a child, I reasoned like a child. When I became a man, I put the ways of childhood behind me. 1 Corinthians 13: 11

**Bible interpretation**

The assumption, a single source is responsible for influences and inaccuracies in western religious beliefs, would underestimate the complexity of our existence. All existing things influence all new things, all natural ... all blameless ... almost always with best intentions. This is human nature, but it has led to our current inaccurately understood paradigms.

Many would like to believe the authors of Christianity existed in a timeless vacuum while creating the religion. This is not only an unreasonable assumption, but psychology declares it humanly impossible. When we delve into the foundational aspects of the Bible, and biblical teaching, we find a far more specific time and place human nature behind the book's perspective and the religion it helped create.

Multiple sources indicate the book's purity has been compromised. Once verified that one part has been compromised, it must be assumed, all parts have been exposed to compromise. Enough information has been verified, to believe the Bible has endured what any piece of influential literature would have endured through this long a course of existence, and psychological perspective reveals flaws in the counter-argument being offered regarding the book's purity. Human tendency is to revere conformity based spirituality without question, but every indication shows, questionable humans held unregulated guardianship of our religious edicts, for longer than our current perspective acknowledges.

This endeavor isn't taken lightly. Finding flaw in such a revered work is painful, but intellectually and scholastically, we should acknowledge that the book reflects human influences from the history of man and the timeline of human knowledge, the history of the religious organization which controlled the Bible documents for ages, the documents' origins, the history of the origin's geographical location, and the history of the specific culture of the people who lived in that part of the world at the time, the history of the places those documents traveled through, the language barriers, the time barriers, the interpretation difficulties, the propensities of the organizations translating the book, the lack of outside objective governance regarding the controlling organization, knowledge of psychology as it pertains to the passage of time, and cultural influence on human existence.

There are/were similar documents, written about the same subjects, during the same time, which were discarded when the

Bible was assembled, and documents have since been discovered, with equivalent time and place authenticity, which have also been unceremoniously discarded.

With these realizations, is it intellectually acceptable to inquire, what rubric was created and used to verify certain documents and eliminate others? The bible was assembled three hundred years after Christ's death. Has anyone in the following seventeen hundred years, questioned the criteria used to authenticate this selection process? We hold this book in the highest reverence, and not only does it receive the least intellectual scrutiny, but people who question it get ignored, ostracized, or threatened with extinction. Why?

How I was led to the validation of my knowledge is equally both self-concerning and perplexing, but I have the knowledge and information I possess, and this document is a small sampling of what I've found. How I've been led to some of the information is peculiar, but the included words and subsequent conclusions can be measured by anyone caring to measure.

http://listverse.com/2013/06/30/ten-influences-on-the-bible/

[ '… the many books that make up the Bible were, in fact, written by a number of different authors, some of whom are unknown. And these men were influenced in a variety of ways. This is in accordance with historical patterns, and connections to older references can be found in almost any other religious and or historical text. Although this topic has been much debated, it's commonly accepted by scholars today that the following parts of the Bible may have been influenced by other cultures:

The Persian scriptures of the Zoroastrians, the Avesta tells the story of how Ormuzd created the world and the first two humans in six days and then rested on the seventh. The names of these two human beings were Adama and Evah. These texts date back as far as the 10th century B.C.

The Story of Noah: A man is warned of an imminent flood by a god and is instructed to build a large boat in order to survive. Though these details sound like they were taken directly from the book of Genesis, you'd find the same information in the story of Utnapishtim, found in the Epic of Gilgamesh.

Proverbs in the bible and the Egyptian Instruction of Amenemope parallel each other.

The Ten Commandments were given to Moses on Mount Sinai and were written on stone tablets, allegedly by the hand of God himself. This was thought to take place around 1490 B.C. However when one examines chapter 125 of the Egyptian Book of the Dead (around 2600 B.C.), it seems he may have had a little help. The Egyptian Book of the Dead reads like the Ten Commandments written in the Negative Confession.

Psalms 29 is a hymn that bears so much similarity to Ugaritic (the language of the Canaanites) poetry that some believe it was originally a hymn to Baal. Today scholars agree that the Israelites emerged from a Canaanite civilization in the early part of the second millennium B.C.

There is an interesting correlation between the Gathas of Zarathushtra Yasna (the sacred texts of the Zoroastrians) and the chapter of creation and book of Isaiah in the Old Testament.

According to scholars, the Zoroastrians were the first to believe in angels, the idea of Satan, and the ongoing battle between the forces of good and evil. Interestingly, Zoroastrian art portrays the prophet Zarathustra as being surrounded by the same halo of light in which Christian figures are often depicted.

The concept of Heaven and Hell seem to predate Judaism as well. Once again, we go back Zoroastrianism and Persian influence. The prophet Daniel was the first biblical figure to refer to ideas of resurrection and judgment in Daniel 12:2, and this can be easily attributed to Babylonian influence. The word "paradise" comes directly from the Persian religion of Mithraism. The word "Hell" seems to derive from the Norse word Hel, most certainly a pre-Christian concept. There are countless examples of Hell-like afterlives portrayed in pagan and Greek mythology.

In the New Testament, there are four different words used to describe Hell, all of which have been translated into English as

"Hell". They are "Sheol", which means "place of the dead"; "Hades," the Greek god of the underworld, "Gehenna," a kind of garbage dump; and "Tartaro," which means "to cast" or "throw".

Examples of pagan trinities are: Amun, Re, and Ptah of Egyptian Mythology; Anu, Enlil, and Ea of Sumerian Mythology; and Ishtar, Baal, and Tammuz of Babylonian Mythology.

There are still some remarkable parallels between the teachings of Jesus and the teachings of Buddha, Mithras, and Zarathustra.

**Jesus:** "And as you would that men should do to you, do you also to them in like manner." (Luke 6:31)
**Buddha:** "Consider others as yourself." (Dhammapada 10:1)

**Jesus:** "And to him that striketh thee on the one cheek, offer also the other. And him that taketh away from thee thy cloak, forbid not to take thy coat also." (Luke 6:29)
**Buddha:** "If anyone should give you a blow with his hand, with a stick, or with a knife, you should abandon any desires and utter no evil words." (Majjhima Nikaya 21:6)' ]

This list omits another unintentional plagiarism: *The Song of Akhenaten*, which predated Psalm 104. Pharaoh Akhenaten, son of Amenhotep, father of Tutankhamun, offered the world the first recorded theory and acknowledgment of a single all-powerful deity (not Abraham), and his ode to this all-powerful being is known as

*The Song of Akhenaten – The great hymn to the Aten.* The words are similar to and precede David's authorship of Psalm 104. - https://www.google.com/search?q=The+Song+of+Akhenaten&oq=The+Song+of+Akhenaten&gs_l=psy-ab.12...0.0.0.140125.0.0.0.0.0.0.0..0.0.foo%2Cersl%3D1%2Cfett%3D1%2Cewh%3D0%2Cnso-enksa%3D0%2Cnso-enfk%3D0...0...1..64.psy-ab..0.0.0.4SxGFklJwdo

Akhenaten's reign was short and unsuccessful and his heir Tutankhamun (King Tut) reverted the kingdom back to multi-theistic worship.

* Western Civilizations   Coffin & Stacey  Vol 1 Pg 47-49, 50

But certain Bible excerpts whether plagiarized or not, have not lost their meaning, and hold great truth.

http://www.aish.com/jl/jnj/jn/48925332.html
by Rabbi Ken Spiro

[     'The Impact of the Bible:  The Bible is the best-selling book in human history. Its moral, spiritual and even political impact has been profound and unmistakable. How did that come to be?'

'…The historical process which led to the mass spread of the Bible…

Our story begins with the spread of Christianity in the Roman Empire. In the 4th century, especially during the reign of Emperor Constantine (306-337 CE), Christianity made the dramatic switch from persecuted splinter sect of Judaism to major world religion. During the following centuries, the Christian faith spread throughout Europe and the Middle East gathering millions of new adherents who were formally pagans.

As the church spread, it grew into a tremendous political and physical power. With the collapse of the Western Roman Empire in 476 CE, the church took over the reigns of authority within former empire boundaries. (2)

At the same time, the collapse of Rome led to a precipitous decline in culture, literacy and general quality of life in the region. Out of this relative chaos emerged the feudal system which would serve as the main political and economic structure of Medieval Europe. Within this feudal system, the church, with its vast network of dioceses, huge land-holdings, and relatively literate clergy, emerged as the most powerful institution. The church's power grew to such an extent that by the 11th century Pope Innocent III was more powerful than any monarch in Europe and church revenues from feudal taxation far exceeded the revenues collected by local nobility and even kings. (3)

Besides physically controlling much of Europe, the church also controlled the spiritual destiny of the Western Christian world and the soul of every Christian. It could grant pardons and offer salvation or punish with excommunication or supposedly, eternal damnation.

The church also had an almost complete monopoly on both literacy and books in Medieval Europe, as the only people who were educated to read were clergy, with very few exceptions. (One such exception were the Jewish, who had a near 100 percent literacy among them.) The reason for this was partly economic. Before the development of the printing press in the 15th century, all books had to be copied by hand, a very time consuming and expensive process. The few libraries that existed were virtually all in the hands of the church and the vast majority of people could neither afford a book nor read one.

The feudal system was a primitive and harsh system. The vast majority of people were peasant farmers who led a subsistence level existence, slaving away on farms and paying most of their meager harvest in taxes to the nobility or the church. The church reaped huge economic benefit from this feudal system yet as it grew in wealth and power it found itself in an uncomfortable moral position.

In theory, Christianity was based on both the teachings of the Hebrew Bible and the Christian Gospels and Writings. The Hebrew Bible constantly speaks about the notions of equality, charity, social responsibility, and spirituality. The Christian Gospels and Writings echo many of the same sentiments and also stress the idea of the meek inheriting the earth. These ethical ideals were in sharp contrast to the realities of the very materialistic and powerful medieval church. This hypocrisy did not escape the church's awareness and thus we have one of the great ironies of history - the Roman Catholic Church which drew its legitimacy directly from the Bible was more afraid of the Bible than any other book in its library!

The church embarked on a deliberate policy to deny the common people access to the Bible. (4) This policy forbade a member of the clergy from owning or publicly reading from the Bible without special permission from higher church officials. Even if a local parish priest was given permission to read the Bible to his flock, every copy was written in Latin, so virtually no peasants would understand what he or she was hearing.

So threatened was the church by the Bible that in 1408 Bishop Arundel of England decreed that anyone making or using an unlicensed translation of the Bible was liable to be put to death. (5)

Persecution of the Bible carried on for centuries...'

SOURCES:

1. Goldberg, M. Hirsh, "Jewish Connection," Maryland: Scarborough House, 1993, pp. 6-130.

2. Johnson, Paul, "A History of Christianity," New York: Simon & Schuster, 1976, p. 104.

3. Dillenberger, John and Welch, Claude, "Protestant Christianity: Interpreted Through Its Development," New York: Charles Scribner and Sons, 1954, p. 11.

4. Phelps-Brown, Henry, "Egalitarianism and the Generation of Inequality," Oxford:Oxford University Press, 1988, p. 68.

5. Tuchman, Barbara, "The Bible and the Sword," New York: New York University Press, 1956, p.85.' ]

Certain religious organizations show a marked separation from Christ's teachings, and these are the people who held unregulated control over Bible content, since its inception.

Saint Thomas Aquinas (AD 13th Century) writings were the first documented turn against LGBT. Before *Saint* Aquinas, LGBT were accepted in many cultures ruled by the church.

Then came the printing press and book mass-reproduction… and the Puritans.

Having been thrown out of Britain for their radical religious beliefs, they landed in New England USA and became a societal and cultural influence…without ever changing their radical beliefs. We are still a puritan influenced society, and dismissing some of our last puritan religious beliefs would probably prove healthy. The other puritan claim to fame: The Salem MA witch trials and murders, for which, no one was ever held responsible.

The American Puritan Ethic and puritan influence are not pure or positive. They have been and continue to be evaluated in our school systems, and it is widely accepted, the Puritan religious point of view is not what the Bible teaches, but like all cultures throughout history, beliefs are melded together from many sources and are seldom singular or pure in concept, interpretation, or application. The Puritans once banned Christmas. It didn't meet their piety standards.

In 1883, under Puritan influence, Miriam Webster of dictionary fame completed what he called his masterpiece: a completely cleaned up version of the Bible. He removed entire chapters proclaiming them too (sexually) filthy for any human being to read. Is your Bible, the Bible of your ancestors? We have Webster's documented proof otherwise.

1946: The year of the introduction of the word *homosexual* in the Bible. It was not found in any previous version. Misinterpretations of the word could fill a book. Matthew 19: 11-12 uses the misinterpretation: eunuch. (Definition of eunuch: Men uncomfortable sleeping with women)

Another interesting fact about Catholicism: Priests were allowed to marry until 1100 ACE. The Vatican decided too much pricey real estate was being inherited by clergy heirs and decided they were no longer allowed to marry. The edict wasn't spiritually inspired, nor is it biblical in origin.

## Re-writings and re-interpretations

By the time the Bible had arrived at Renaissance enlightenment, it had already been in the autonomous control of questionable people for roughly twelve hundred years, and there are many indications, many of the book's original messages had been compromised. There is indication it once included dragons and unicorns in the original King James version. The original creation story has God fighting an equally powerful ocean dragon, for reigning control of Earth (which was then considered the entirety of sentient existence).

(book:)

*The Circulation of Roman Catholic Versions of the Bible by the British and Foreign Bible Society*:

The Defense of the Practice, examined by a Clergyman of the Church of England

**January 1, 1868**

https://books.google.com/books?id=UelUAAAAcAAJ&pg=PA24&lpg=PA24&dq=The+Bible:+Who+wrote+%27Romans%27?&source=bl&ots=gooaX3Nzt4&sig=hOvwp-XDuhok_9WLlLF3mGcrul0&hl=en&sa=X&ved=0ahUKEwj-gJjp09TVAhXJ4iYKHfr5ALwQ6AEIczAR#v=onepage&q=The%20Bible%3A%20Who%20wrote%20%27Romans%27%3F&f=false

[ Pg 18

3. 'We now come from admissions to facts, and give more proof that something essential in involved.

The atonement of our Lord Jesus – one sacrifice once offered in an essential doctrine of Christianity. But its denial is involved in the "unduly biased" translations of Gen. xiv 17-19; Matt xxvi 28; Mark xiv 24; Luke xxii 20; 1 Cor. x. 16; xi 24; Eph. iii. 3. 4; and 1 Tim iii. 16; from which the Romanists deduce "the sacrifice of the Mass" and "Transubstantiation."

The worship of God only, is an essential doctrine. He declares, "Mine honor I will not give to another." But its denial is involved in the "mistranslations" of Gen. iii. 15; Exod. xx. 5; Job. V. 1; Ps. xcviii. 5; Luke 1. 28; John ii. 4; Col. ii. 18; Heb. xi. 21; from which Romans deduce the dogma of the worship of the Blessed Virgin and created things.

Justification by faith is an essential doctrine. But its denial is involved in the Roman doctrine of "good works", which is proved from the "mistranslation" of Deut. xxiv. 13; Dan iv. 27; Eph. ii. 10; Phil. iv. 17,18; Philem. 22; Heb. xiii. 16; and 2 Pet. i. 10; Rev. iii. 3,4; xix. 8.

Repentance—a change of mind and heart …utterly perverted by the mistranslation of …

In addition to these, we have Purgatory, proved by the Romanists by the insertion of "to stop" in Luke xvi. 28; and from 1 Pet. iii. 19.

4. The errors are not trivial or microscopic. ....' ]

That last line isn't my thought. It is the thought of the clergy author(s): circa 1868, who produced the book referenced above.

Information supporting this argument exists throughout the period when refuting argument was acceptable. There are historical reasons why refuting evidence doesn't exist before a certain date. Anyone familiar with the atrocities of human religious history also knows. The reasons aren't secret. Whether you choose to accept them, is a topic for a separate discussion.

Imprisonment and murder were common for people getting in the way of certain earthly religious agendas. And this circumstance is more current than anyone would think. The Lebanon incident occurring during the late 1970's, is an uncomfortably current example.

So who added 'to stop' to Luke and created Purgatory? Then who destroyed it? The Sacred word of God, seems to change with human manipulation.

Did a religion make an entire spiritual realm appear, then disappear? Is this religious paradigm readjustment unprecedented or is this an example of religious authority adjusting its founding content whenever inclined? Are actions like this supposed to go unnoticed? Were those who had the ability to make like adjustments in the past, aware they operated with impunity, because they were aware they had ultimate authority, even over 'God's own words'?

I imagine many humans worked diligently to keep the Bible pure and without mistranslation, but that doesn't mean they succeeded, or started with the original documents (or facts). And original documentation doesn't mean the messages weren't misinterpreted due to the place, time, and method of interpretation.

The interpretation of Sodom and Gomorrah was once believed to rail against homosexuality, with a supposedly deviant sexual act being named after the fallen city. Most religious now believe the story is about greed and excess, and nothing to do with the puritan misinterpretation of sexual misconduct. That interpretation speaks more about the interpreter than the Bible message, but countless humans suffered and died due to the Bible's immature human interpretation.

I petition we use the above arguments, to understand humans misrepresent many of God's intentions and messages, and need to re-evaluate perpetuating the notion that past antiquated questionable beliefs are the answer for the human race moving forward. Don't you think it is time we acknowledge and dismiss past inaccuracies and move forward as the more universally aware beings we profess we are?

To those denying others based on Bible authority, without verifying interpretation, below is one example of an original Bible message *currently* inaccurately believed to be the 'silver bullet, killing all LGBT.

Please note how the original message spoke somewhat transcendentally and how the misinterpretation not only fails the original message due to not-so-hidden human agendas, but manages to abuse the exact groups the original message meant to protect. The misinterpretation causes the exact opposite message. Not a slightly inaccurate message. The *exact* opposite message.

1 Corinthians 6: 9

https://www.biblegateway.com/passage/?search=1+Corinthians+6%3A9&version=NIV

[  ⁹ Or do you not know that wrongdoers will not inherit the kingdom of God? Do not be deceived: Neither the sexually immoral nor idolaters nor adulterers nor men who have sex with men[a]

> \* **Footnotes:**
> a. 1 Corinthians 6:9: The words *men who have sex with men* translate two Greek words that refer to the passive and active participants in homosexual acts. ]

\* This footnote is in the notes on the Bible website and **not my footnote**.

- Operative Greek words in the original Greek document: "Malakoi" and "Arsenkoitai":

   \* *THESE* are the two Greek words the footnote references.

— Malakoi 's literal translation means 'weak willed' / 'gutless' / 'spineless' …was somehow **mistranslated** to: effeminate …as in sexually / genderly effeminate / gay / lgbt

— Arsenkoitai : Modern humans cannot find a literal translation for this highly uncommon and rare Greek word, but to declare its meaning: 'homosexuality' is once again more an adage against the interpreter than the Bible meaning. There were, at the time of original authorship, many words which meant 'homosexual' in the Greek language and if that's what the author wanted to convey, it is believed he would have used one of those many common words. He did not.

A re-translation *still* not befitting a Perfect God and Her Unconditional love/forgiveness, but at least without a human death-toll…

'Or do you not know that wrongdoers will not inherit the kingdom of God? Do not be deceived: Neither the morally weak-willed, nor people who fail to defend those being oppressed.'

So a half-wise argument for standing up *to* bullies – in all their singular and multi-human combinations - and a discourse against being gutless and weak willed, as upstanding Christians … a rally cry for defending those who need defending—turned into a twisted rant *against* the oppressed, and a natural human sexual individuality?

But either way, who is this author who thinks he has the authority to judge the eternal destination of human beings, when the Bible clearly states in multiple places, no human has the authority to judge humans spiritually? That includes Bible authors, because Bible authors were human. This bible author has no authority over, or input into who inherits the Kingdom of God. God decides who inherits the Kingdom of God.

Or is the interpreter/interpretation flawed? God isn't flawed, so there's an obvious spiritual disconnect between God and the author, or his message.

There are many misinterpreted messages, and humans have a choice. We can either identify who is spiritually misguided, or eliminate statements like this from our *good book* so we can progress to the next level of sentient understanding.

Others can't find flaws in the Bible, but I can't accidentally *not* find argument the book is flawed. God is perfect. If a bible passage isn't, it means the bible passage is of human influence or origin.

What the author or interpreter didn't understand is, how God teaches and how lessons are shared. It is enclosed.

Accident or not, I find myself doing as Paul the Apostle seemed to backwardly petition in his *original* message. I'm standing up for humans, against existing social and cultural paradigms currently perpetuating abuse without intellectual foundation. Some things decreed in the Bible do nothing more than solicit human common sense, decency, and consideration. Some Bible messages also call for action.

Those same messages are also found in every religion around the world. They are not holy or religious. They're calls for common human decency and discourse. (love/forgive?)

And we find, those who should be preaching the lessons loudest, are the exact ones preaching against the message, the loudest. Why?

When a religion or preacher uses a bible message to preach the opposite of unquestionable unconditional love, scrutinize the messenger. More than likely you'll find a less-than-Godly human behind the religiously-confusing sermon. If you associate success with truth, please understand, the two concepts are not positively correlated in any aspect of existence.

Two-thousand years past the most famous western-world petition for common human decency (The Bible) - being misinterpreted and manipulated in a way that compounds the human error to its greatest extent. Like 1 Corinthians 6:9 and Sodom and Gomorrah, humans are using Bible messages in exactly the opposite way they were intended.

With regard to both the Sodom and Gomorrah, and Corinthians stories - the compound error: We're not only oppressing innocent humans, but by not taking the time to truly interpret the original messages, without prejudice, we're allowing unscrupulous people to surreptitiously abuse groups of people which the actual original messages asked us to defend. By sharing and perpetuating unverified hearsay, we also fail to share the original concepts of some of the actual original stories.

~~~

"Tell me again how you think GOD will judge others for who they love and not judge you for hating someone you've never met?" – Laverne Cox

During a certain *translation/interpretation period*, it seems the Bible translators were more than a little sexually obsessed, as if the Bible was nothing more than an anti-sex manual. One author even extolls the virtues of celibacy over marriage. History suggests he was married. We will never know the reasoning behind his opinion, but understand how different it is from Godly:

God gave humans – seven – innate inherent pleasures. One of them is sexual orgasm. This is a gift from God. A person of authority suggesting celibacy is more Godly, would indicate a lack of spiritual maturity and understanding.

For an organization to include such information in a religious book, and for others to accept and perpetuate the notion, would show additional examples of spiritual immaturity. How accurate is this opinion? Intelligent people have been ignoring this 'wisdom' for as long as this wisdom has existed. Do you ignore this wisdom?

You may have or may develop any view you wish, to get through this point of your existence. You may also have your opinion on how your choice is better than other opinions, and need to deny yourself all you need to 'sacrifice', to get to your nirvana. Please do, but please don't think others need be as mature or aware as you. Your choices are yours, as mine are only mine. To refuse to recognize differing opinions on this or any subject, does nothing more than declare your level of maturity.

Have the convictions of your personal beliefs based on your knowledge and experience. If they lead to conclusions regarding your freedoms, then by all means don't let someone else dictate your servitude, and please don't force your personal convictions on others.

And please remember, your personal freedoms shouldn't abuse, harm, or oppress anyone. Those are freedoms we don't have authority over.

The perplexing part of this dialog is, this immature cultural sexual obsession continues today, though those perpetuating the mindset don't necessarily personally adhere to their anti-sexual societal opinions or messages. There are countless clergy / preachers / religious affiliated leaders, who have been caught breaking their / their organizations' anti-sexual rules. Currently, the number of religious pedophiles alone, outnumber the clergy/preachers we would like to believe make up the entirety of those who can't seem to adhere to their own sexually repressive messages.

The idea religious organizations not only protect these humans, but also empower them to abuse by hiding their identities or transferring them to unknowing jurisdictions, show how disconnected religious organizations and God are.

There is a large religiously affiliated street billboard in an adjoining town, which asks a question proposed by a person who claims the title of 'doctor': 'Does sex tell the truth or lies?'

Answer: It does neither. Sex isn't a living thinking entity, and the idea someone anthropomorphizes sex – (the projection of living traits and emotions on non-living things) indicates a very young mentality. Psychology has put a very young mental/emotional age on those practicing this level of mindset.

People able to maturely reason, know this, but most have decided against speaking out. Speaking out jeopardizes our safety. Why? What is wrong with offering a different though unpopular awareness? Why is it not wrong, denying someone that freedom? How is mindless conformity better, for the growth of humanity?

The billboard author gave two choices as if our choice was only one of two answers – and this is the current religious mindset we negotiate daily.

No third option. One or the other.

We're being asked to choose between conforming to religious childishness, or risking eternal damnation. Did you ever listen to young sibling children talk to each other when a parent can't be seen?

…But there are more than two options. In fact, the third option not mentioned by our religious, or this specific billboard author, is the actual only option: Consensual sex is natural, often highly pleasurable, and a gift from your Perfect Creator, who loves you unconditionally.

You have a Perfect Spiritual Mother/Father who has declared you Her/His child and if you're not sure, I've written one hell of an argument.

We're also aware of the specific cultural values the religious authors sanctioned with regard to gender equality, and their mindset caught in their time and place of existence, extended well past their time of existence. One of the supposed great religious thinkers in Christian history – St. Thomas Aquinas (circa AD 1250) – perpetuated the original male / female inequality …

- "…As regards the individual nature, woman is defective and misbegotten, for the active power of the male seed tends to the production of a perfect likeness in the masculine sex; while the production of a woman comes from defect in the active power...." Thomas Aquinas, Summa Theologica, Q92, art. 1

Aquinas is not only considered a great religious thinker, but was declared a 'saint'. If I read his words without knowing authorship, I'd swear he was clueless with regard to who God is or how God works. In actuality, he was no more than a product of his time and place of earthly existence. It's easy to see. His words are his mindset ...his lack of spirituality is easily viewed and unmistakably evident. ...A saint, considered one of the great Christian thinkers.

Such past immaturity would be acceptable, if religions would acknowledge their time and place limitations, but Mr. Aquinas wasn't the last religious human to declare these antiquated beliefs valid. Every Pope since has perpetuated the immaturity, including the current human holding the position.

Dear Pontiff, are you God's representative? If yes, when do you declare it with action befitting God? Female and male are equal. Declare it. Be so brave as to declare it with action*. Do you truly not see it, or do you also know it, but cower to your organization?

* And to paraphrase a past President ... I will attend the mass of the first married lesbian female priest.

Dear Pontiff, the child that becomes this person, is God's child, like you and I are God's children.

I don't believe anyone purposefully plagiarized or misinterpreted the stories in the Bible. Stories are easily and innocently adopted. A twenty-century long human quotient went into the creation and constant interpretation of the Bible and other religious books, and they haven't been re-evaluated because those who hold the book(s) most sacred, believe they are transcendentally sacred, written by God, above reproach, and don't need further evaluation. I appreciate the sentiment, but with study, understand the inaccuracy.

Psychology states, all human endeavor, even that which is destructive, is done to enhance one's own life and if possible, the lives of others. And bad decisions are misguided or misinformed attempts to do good.

Yes, every once in a while, good people are mistaken and do misguided things. It is almost never intentional. No one means to deceive for evil reasons. Almost no humans exist under those terms, and the four-tenths of one percent which do, do not register here for this intellectual discussion.

But searching the internet for any one Bible verse, helps illuminate human limitations translating the book. The sheer number of Bible versions based on interpretation, explains how many attempts at Bible translation exist, and how easy it is to take a simple verse and turn it into twenty-five similar, but noticeably different meanings ...and this is for one single human language:

Young's Literal Translation / World English Bible / Weymouth New Testament / Webster's Bible Translation / English Revised Version / Darby Bible Translation / Douay-Rheims Bible / American Standard Version / American King James Version / King James 2000 Bible / Jubilee Bible 2000 / New American Standard 1977 / GOD'S WORD® Translation / Aramaic Bible in Plain

English / New Heart English Bible / NET Bible / International Standard Version / Holman Christian Standard Bible / King James Bible / New American Standard Bible / Berean Literal Bible / Berean Study Bible / English Standard Version / New Living Translation / New International Version

    Another seemingly ignored translation / interpretation aspect is the lack of concern for the accreditation of the individuals or groups of individuals doing the translating and interpreting. Please note, there were no standards for the process, or verifications after the process. Entities sold their finished product after they produced it. There was no further concern for accuracy, and the producing entities had many time and place proclivities which influenced their particular versions.

    Consider how time has had the same ill-effect on meaning and translation. Modern English-speaking school students think Shakespeare is written in a different language and though English teachers take offense to the notion, the students are right. If the words aren't easily comprehended – as written, and the language needs translating, even if the language is supposedly the one being spoken, then the document being read isn't the current understood language. – By syllogistic definition -a foreign language. If it is not the familiar language, then it is foreign (look up a larger definition of *foreign*).

Rules don't supersede common sense, no matter how many English teachers insist otherwise. Now do this with every language, through two-thousand years, and see if a message or two doesn't go awry.

More on the add-ons, inaccuracies, and omissions in the Bible:

http://www.newsweek.com/2015/01/02/thats-not-what-bible-says-294018.html

We've established, some Bible stories have possibly been misinterpreted and or manipulated beyond their original messages. A new perspective and reframing of old stories will offer a new potential, where old perspectives fall short of their intended prospective.

Reframing: A psychological tool which helps humans understand different standpoints of the same stimulus. (action)

The first stories in the Bible, our ancestors, their condemning actions, and the first insight into primitive views of God have already been reframed, and the reframing now fits within natural and acceptable modern intellectual boundaries worthy of a perfect spiritual Being who exists perfectly, loves perfectly / unconditionally, and forgives perfectly.

Gilgamesh's and Noah's flood is mentioned in historical documents around the world, including the Aztecs, China, India, Russia, Scandinavia, and Wales. And since these documents and their people survived the ordeal, either God had a lot of people building arks in all different places, or … The earth flooded and some people survived. It floods and lights on fire every so many thousand years. Floods, meteors (fire and brimstone), hurricanes, earthquakes, and volcanos are naturally occurring events, not spiritual edicts. We live on a volatile planet, which passes through some debris-strewn sections of space; new space regularly, like the orbit of a spirograph toy. We do not have an angry, vindictive Creator.

The further back in history one studies, the more frequently, attempted anthropomorphism and connections to otherworldly origins and edicts, epic events become. The assumption, people who lived two thousand years ago had the same intellectual wherewithal, universal understanding, and worldliness as people living today, is inaccurate.

They lived and were ruled under different physical, intellectual, spiritual, and emotional levels of awareness, and their standards are immeasurably antiquated compared to modern life two thousand years or thirteen hundred years later, depending on which uneducated myopic religiously-based culture you want to measure modern man against.

The first distant galaxies outside the Milky Way were discovered in 1930. Our current perspective is immeasurably beyond the perceptions of one hundred years ago. Now multiply that difference by twenty.

Those who still want to hold to two thousand year old edicts may prove so by throwing away their phones and selling their cars. Otherwise, please smile and join the rest of us on this fascinating journey.

Everything in Biblical times had religious or spiritual connotations. It was their way of life and a reflection of their society and culture; not a reflection of a perfect unconditionally loving God. May we begin to recognize the difference?

If Biblical decrees don't reflect perfect unconditional love … if they seem trite and concerned with minutiae, they are of human origin; no matter how many times the authors or leaders swears the edict came from God's direct communication.

God, as I've been made aware, has no direct input in minutiae, and the only measurement method I can think of, to measure unidentified spiritual advisors is: Are the messages love/forgive, or are they hate? We can use the same measurement criteria for every concept presented in our religious literature.

God offers no direct communication. Humans couldn't endure direct communication from God. God's spirit / aura doesn't physically allow it. There is a hierarchy of governance and communication within the spirit world, just like here on earth. We get our concepts of governance systems from the original universe. We also interact (and sometimes communicate) with the entities assigned us. And they answer to whom they answer, and so on…

This is paradigm-shifting, and it's okay if you're not ready to digest it. The truth seems to have little personal significance other than making the path ahead existentially congruent.

Believing a literal translation of the Bible means, Sodom and Gomorrah's fire and brimstone was a direct edict from God, but a similar fireball lighting up Chicago in 1871, or the two fireballs that hit Siberia within the last hundred years were just natural events? God was amazingly hands-on and rather picayune for eons— during the period when communication verification was impossible, but now He's taking a two-thousand year nap, and thank goodness. Every one of His supposed biblical interactions are horrendous. For a biblical Creator God who is unconditional love, no one has a story of Him doing anything loving without horrible ramifications. If you *'believe'*: the story of His greatest act of love, tortured and killed his Son in one of the most gruesome deaths imaginable.

Or…

God doesn't interact physically with humans, and the stories of horror don't have His signature on them. Humans are more in charge of and responsible for our actions and fate than we want to admit, and we *do* know the difference between right and wrong, and have the ability to act maturely or immaturely. The actual issue: We choose poorly too often. We choose to act immaturely, too often.

This book offers ideas on how to change the percentage of poor and immature choices. There's a chance we make some poor decisions based on the idea, it is who our Creator is, and we're emulating Him. This book attempts to readjust that mentality, hoping humans will continue to try to emulate God, by changing their mindset, after adjusting their perception of God.

Christ taught love. In word and action. Only love. God is love. In word and action. Only love. To believe otherwise is inaccurate.

"And you shall know the truth and the truth shall make you free." John 8:32

...and if you're not free ...maybe you don't know the truth (syllogistic logic)

Jesus says: "My yoke is easy and my burden light." Mat 11:30

If your spiritual yoke isn't easy or your burden light, maybe your beliefs are inaccurate. Are you less or more burdened by what you're currently being taught by your current spiritual institutions? Are you being taught anything making you uncomfortable intellectually, emotionally, socially, or spiritually?

Christ may or may not have died on a cross, but why should it matter? If He is God, then He is God. He didn't become God *after* dying on the cross. He is God or He isn't, well before he became man.

"In the beginning was the Word, and the Word was with God" John 1:1

Whether God or man, the words attributed to Christ are often brilliant, and if we honored His words and wishes, the earth would be the garden we swear we were expelled from. I would suggest those who 'believe' without ever having read a word attributed to this impressive teacher, do so. My favorite line attributed to him:

[34]A new command I give you. Love one another. As I have loved you, so you must love one another. [35]By this everyone will know you are my disciples, if you love one another. John 13: 34-35

Confirmation that reading and honoring Christ's words mean more than believing blindly and contradicting His teachings:

[3] We know that we have come to know him if we keep his commands. [4] Whoever says, "I know him," but does not do what he commands is a liar, and the truth is not in that person. 1 John 2:3-4

The above verse does not translate to 'The Ten Commandments'. It refers to Christ's teachings; especially His command to love (John 13: 34-35 Read it again). Please consider giving His teachings more attention. May I suggest you study His words as if you're a student, not peruse as if reading for pleasure. The people I've shown John 13 34-35 have all told me they've read it but never paused to truly appreciate it for its significance.

Stipulation: If the words attributed Christ do not strictly adhere to the rest of His message, please understand there is a chance the outlier message may have been misinterpreted or misconstrued through the myriad of means mentioned previously. He is perfect love from perfect love. Any message contradicting that fact, needs re-examining.

# Chapter Eight
## Law vs Love

**LAW**

All existence operates under one rule. Love/Forgive. Love over law. Yet the earth still wishes to consider law over love. Earth's problems don't stem from specific human acts that bear no hatred. Earth's dilemma is its choice to adhere to religious laws long ago destroyed; to adhere to law over love. Many of Earth's problems can be explained by that short phrase: law over love.

Our self-imposed restrictions.

Our self-restriction lists differ in every culture, and change like blowing sand. Some cultures have more than one set of human restrictions. Example: Western culture has its current secular, and antiquated religious laws.

Most human restrictions are put in place as a culture matures. This list doesn't mature with the maturing culture. Usually, the opposite process develops, or cultural collapse wouldn't be the norm. We understand where restrictions come from and why certain restrictions are necessary, but most of us can name more than one senseless restriction for every sensible one.

Since we're discussing proposed religious restrictions/laws, and their origin, we can focus on what destroys them, for this discussion. Questionable secular restrictions can be discussed at another time.

Laws…even those supposedly written in stone, should be evaluated regularly for social maturity and intelligence. The psychological theory behind this axiom is Kohlberg's Moral Reasoning Theory. It is foundational and highly strategic during an evaluation process. This theory positively correlates to the Gautama quote – Question Everything – which has been discussed.

Cultural mores are formed through human intellect and time constrained. Love/forgive is wisdom based, and transcends time and place.

Individually, certain people like to hold personally invented self-restrictions against others, sometimes *all* others. It's a trait most inadequate leaders possess.

Old religious laws have been declared dead since (and if you believe - through) Christ. If you refuse to leave them dead, they revive as your personal master. Others aren't obligated to adhere to them. If you revive* them, they're yours and yours alone. Please stop pretending others must adhere to your laws or your inability to understand who your laws affect.

Some won't understand, and will explain that off unless I explain further.

Galatians 3: 10 states:

[10]All who rely on observing the law are **under a curse**, for it is written: "Cursed is everyone who does not continue to do *everything* written in the Book of the Law."

\* If you declare another – subject to a religious law, and hold that law against them – you then must adhere to *all* religious law. In order to hold a law against another, you must believe it law. If you declare one law which you can adhere to – law others must adhere to – you must adhere to *ALL* Law, including those you cannot adhere to. And thusly, you have cursed you. You are loved unconditionally but actions have circumstances.

Love and you're shown love. Forgive and you're forgiven. Judge and you are judged. Judge religiously …and you've cursed yourself.

**LAW versus LOVE**

**LOVE**

I have my opinions on the results attained by replacing law with love. I watched an earthly father refuse to do anything but love his children, even when they were bad, and when they became old enough to realize their father loved them to that degree, they began behaving in response to his love. Meanwhile, as they aged, everyone questioned his method. His method was based on multiple reasons. He watched his father physically abuse his brothers, under the punishment scheme of obeyance. One brother (who hated his father) grew into an exact copy of the father, and no longer has a relationship with one of his sons.

Rules or Love. You reap what you sow. You model those you observe.

Rules can replace certain aspects of love, but don't think rules are an adequate conformity replacement for love or that love doesn't work as well as rules. Christ asked people to follow Him using Love, and twelve men not only did Christ's work, but supposedly ended up dying for Him. Love conforms better than rules ever could or will.

Discipline is a derivative of 'disciple', and teaches a much deeper level of conformity, than law and punishment. There is an article which explains the difference, written by Bruno Bettelheim: *Punishment vs Discipline*. It is in the April 1985 edition of Atlantic Magazine. The article explains the difference between punishment and discipline, through a unique perspective.

I've shown you the *Love Verse* from Corinthians 13: 4-8, 13

"Love is patient, love is kind. It does not envy, it does not boast, it is not proud. It does not dishonor others, it is not self-seeking, it is not easily angered, it keeps no record of wrongs. Love does not delight in evil but rejoices with the truth. It always protects, always trusts, always hopes, always perseveres. Love never fails. ... And now these three remain: faith, hope and love. But the greatest of these is love."

John 13: 34-35 [34] "A new command I (Christ) give you: Love one another. As I have loved you, so you must love one another. [35] By this everyone will know that you are my disciples, if you love one another."

1 John 4: 7-8 [7] Dear friends, let us love one another, for love comes from God. Everyone who loves has been born of God and knows God. [8] Whoever does not love does not know God, because God is love.

1 John 4:11-12 [11] Dear friends, since God so loved us, we also ought to love one another. [12] No one has ever seen God; but if we love one another, God lives in us and his love is made complete in us.

John 4: 19-21 [19] We love because he first loved us. [20] Whoever claims to love God yet hates a brother or sister is a liar. For whoever does not love their brother and sister, whom they have seen, cannot love God, whom they have not seen. [21] And he has given us this command: Anyone who loves God must also love their brother and sister."

John 14: 16 "God is love. Whoever lives in love lives in God, and God in them."

Is love simple or easy? Oh, just the opposite.

It is easy to hate and it is difficult to love. This is how the whole scheme of things works. All good things are difficult to achieve, and bad things are very easy to attain. – Confucius

Love leaves one vulnerable in a world that destroys the vulnerable. It is compassion, caring, genuineness, sympathy and empathy. It is everything said in the Corinthians excerpt above. It is overwhelming, takes courage, leaves one exposed, unprotected, sometimes looking weak or foolish. It takes chances, sometimes against 'good sense'. It includes and welcomes. It reaches out whether first or in return. It not only accepts differences, it celebrates differences. It treats no one as a lesser entity. It takes individuals out-of-their-way to correct wrongs.

Sometimes the negative cost to love is great. But it is all you imagine you would like your God to be. It is all you would be if you were perfect. Now rejoice. It is exactly who our God is, and what He is teaching us to become.

...and to paraphrase a quote from a book I enjoy: 'It is better ...far better, to love completely wrong, then it is to hate completely right.'

May God someday ask you, "Why did you love?"

Don't worry about the answer. If God asks you that question, you already answered correctly.

There are religions which believe, if we learn the lessons taught on Earth, we won't have to repeat this level of learning again. And if we learn them well enough, we might graduate to the next level of existence.

Understand, whatever level of lesson comprehension you're at, is acceptable. You don't have to learn the lessons or be interested in learning lessons. You can repeat this trip as often as you like, but also understand somewhere along the journey, you'll receive lessons, and when the powers-that-be decide it's time to learn...you will. In the meantime, feel free to ride this continual loop roller-coaster until *you're blue. The amusement park entry fee has been paid.

*You do understand you don't come back as 'you', don't you?

It is said, Mother Teresa came to hate God for the atrocity she witnessed and felt compelled to administer. Do you think for a second, God doesn't think she is one of His most beautiful children? She learned to love, to a level of obligation. Very few of us will attain that level. She is God's. Her actions proved it, beyond doubt.

If we have no peace, it is because we have forgotten that we belong to each other. - Mother Teresa

# Chapter Nine
## If God is Perfect...

**Why are children born sick? Why do young people die? Why are there wars, hunger, disease, atrocities?**

Like everything else in our complicated existence, this is complicated. But it's not hard to understand. The beginning of the answer will seem like I misunderstood my own heading. I didn't. I just have to start in a place you didn't know I had to start, so I'm explaining I know where I'm starting and it's part of the answer.

**Reincarnation**

Many religions believe in reincarnation. Buddhism and specifically Siddhartha Gautama, the Buddha (which means: Enlightened one), and the Christ (which means: Anointed One) spoke more about reincarnation than many believe. Many living during their eras didn't understand the concept due to the lack of philosophical and spiritual understanding during their time and place of physical existence.

All of Christ's inferences regarding reincarnation were omitted from Bible manuscripts, except one. One cryptic message was missed and is still in the Bible. No one understands it, so it is well ignored.

Mat 16: 28

"Truly I tell you, some who are standing here will not taste death before they see the Son of Man coming in his kingdom."

Why reincarnation is dismissed as if it is preposterous and why I believe it's very real:

It has been dismissed because neither great mind spoke to people who could or wanted to believe it. I don't believe they failed to explain it. I'm sure they explained it just like I'm about to. I know the Christ did. That has been shared. I'm more inclined to believe those they told, couldn't comprehend. Their time of existence made concepts like this hard to comprehend. This is corroborated by the masses not comprehending Gautama's full reincarnation message.

Both great minds were working with audiences who had a much smaller universal understanding. We can comprehend the concept better now, because we're more aware of the vastness and complexity of existence. Scientists now confirm multi-universe potential.

I've been shown the spiritual universe with its extensive governance. Heaven is not a planet, nor will it be this planet 'when Kingdom comes'. It is a universe, not only currently existing, but in existence long before this physical universe came to be. I'm lead to believe it is the first, oldest, and most vast universe. I've been led to understand it is the origin and end realm for all beings. All beings originate there and are born into other universes. All beings return there after finite based learning experiences culminate.

I've been given a glimpse of my being before I was sent here. I've been told the date of my return to physical mortality. 2213. I share these experiences as a way to frame the following…

We have established that if God the Creator came into being the day He created this universe, She is fourteen billion (Earth) years old …minimum. It's a ridiculous assumption, but it gives us a number preposterous enough to make my point.

Do you really believe a Being who has lived that long and seen that much, would in any way believe fifty to one-hundred years of physical existence is enough to teach a being the definition of existence? Fourteen billion — to eighty years. Die young and you get a ratio of fourteen billion — to thirty? How about those who die very young? Fourteen billion — to fourteen? …Seven?

Do the math by lifetimes instead of years, and let's call one-hundred years a lifetime. One-hundred-forty million lifetimes — to one. Fifty year human life equals two-hundred-eighty million lifetimes — to one. Over a quarter *billion* to one.

One lifetime, no matter how long, teaches one perspective, from one viewpoint, about one human, during one time, with one set of skills, one family, and one set of experiences. Does that sound like a perfect God's idea of how to teach Her children what being alive is about? Is that enough time to experience all there is to experience?

Two of the most brilliant humans ever to walk Earth shared the idea, reincarnation is real. I know I definitely don't fit into ANY of their categories, but for some reason, I was explained what reincarnation means, and I was told the Christ spoke about it.

Physical death doesn't kill us. The Bible supposedly spoke of a second death to fear. Spiritual death. The act of being an immortal sentient being — to non-existence. We are told to fear the concept of that death, but that enlightenment lends itself to the idea, there is more to our existence than this current physical life.

And short of that fate, we have ours: A continual immortal existence involving more mortal lifetimes than we'd want to count; each time, experiencing another existence as another being, whether human or otherwise, whether on this planet or not, whether growing in knowledge or wisdom or not (life-experiencing existence teaches even without lessons) … until we've lived enough lifetimes to truly understand what living, and experiencing is. And then, hopefully then, we'll be a wise and knowledgeable enough spirit to commune with other brilliant, perfect unconditionally loving forgiving beings.

Gautama explained it right, but the many he explained it to, didn't understand. Christ explained it, but one small group led by one emperor unable to understand and accept, chose not to allow the message past their watch.

Gautama's message was twisted over time to put a merit on what physical animal is our next fate. There are ramifications to actions, but existence merit wasn't part of the original message, just as it wasn't part of Christ's or this current attempt at explanation.

You will live and experience a million lifetimes. You will be a million different beings. You will be every color, size, shape …every gender …you'll be every level of success, beauty, physical health, emotional, spiritual, mental and social status and maturity; all under the premise – you'll be experiencing everything a living being can experience.

The concept, humans are finished living after eighty years is an antiquated immature mindset. Not only did the two greatest minds teach differently, but logic would argue their concepts of multiple lives as well.

The idea of one perspective only, for our entire existential life experience, has no place in a more modern concept of true infinite existence, not unlike our planet being the center of the universe, and the earth being the final destination of the spiritual kingdom.

When humans fathomed only their little world, we couldn't comprehend anything outside it. As our vastness increases, so do concepts once too vast for our limited comprehension. We now understand there are more galaxies than we once thought stars, and this new awareness, established using new scientific equipment breakthroughs, is less than one hundred years old.

Can you understand the incalculability of spiritual existence? You've heard the antiquated stories and their accompanying words. ...World without end... They are ancient words from Christianity's creed. But when the thought was created, the author didn't know the word *universe*. The word and its subsequent thought didn't exist yet.

Eighty years? One life perspective and then heaven on the same little ball of insignificant dirt? Does that, matched with the ever-expanding theorems of quantum physics, really represent the potential our scientific community has now revealed?

We don't exist for one lifetime. Our billions-year-old Creator doesn't think that small. Only antiquated humans can.

Is there anything on earth that can prove we can be born after death, and this can happen easily and repeatedly?

Every plant seed must die before it is reborn. If a seed doesn't die, it rots instead of germinating when it becomes wet, and produces nothing. If a seed dries and dies, it can germinate. There isn't one example of this – there are thousands, if not millions.

With that framework, we can address the answer to the original question: Why do atrocities happen? For instance, why do babies die?

So the baby and the parents experience that particular experience, for that particular existence.

Is it awful experiencing it? You bet! Awful! Putrid! Curse God if you're inclined! He can handle it. He knows you're hurting. He knows He crushed you, and you hate Him at that moment. You may hate Him for the rest of that current existence. He understands so much that He doesn't mind you calling Him what you need to call Him. Some experiences call for that, and God knows it. God knows everything. He invented the experience and knows what it feels like. And after you've experienced that experience…so do you.

(It hurt writing that. Stark reality can hurt beyond description.)

And then later, whether a long or short time later (or ever), forgive yourself, then if you're inclined, tell God you're sorry for the hatred you felt and showed, even if you don't feel completely sorry, and then later, tell God you really are sorry—if you reach that point, but He hurt you so deeply. And then understand God loves you and you were forgiven as you were cursing Him, because God is pure perfect love. Do you think such a perfect all-knowing Being would not understand? Not forgive Her children who had to experience such devastating unbearable pain?

And if you don't or can't forgive God for sharing that experience with you …He loves and cares for you just the same, as I was shown when I called Him 'fucking disgusting', with all my heart, and He sent three messengers to come get me and show me He loves me more than I could ever imagine, and the information I based that opinion on, was incorrect. And God did this while I hated Him. And my hate was genuine.

And you and your baby are fine …forever. You and your baby have the ultimate spiritual parent. And we will learn lessons, good and bad, against our will, by the awful grace of God, just as Aeschylus said, two thousand five hundred years ago.

Why is there pain? Because pain is something to experience. Heartache, happiness, love, hate, death, life, success, failure …Ecclesiastes …a time for everything under heaven. But different than taught or thought. It was believed, you would experience some, and others would experience other things. Instead, you will live it all; just not in this lifetime.

Does this mean God doesn't love you more than you can possibly understand? Just the opposite. God knows nothing can harm you. Physical death can't harm us, and God knows it. God loves you, made you immortal, and wants us to experience everything under heaven… everything there is to experience…and we will.

Shall I confound parochial thinkers further? – Every sexual orientation also! You will be and experience every gender and every sexual preference.

It's time to increase our understanding, maturity, and acceptance.

There's another reason why this is our existence: We, and all spirits, have no wants or needs in the spirit world. There are no wants or needs in the spirit world. And because beings in the spirit world experience and feel no experiences, there is no learning in the spirit realm. It is said many places in our wisdom and religious books, or by people who have experienced the spiritual realm: There is nothing but an amazing all-encompassing love, peace, and a feeling, you want for nothing …for nothing, in that universe. And that also teaches *nothing*.

So for you as a being, and the cosmos as an entity which seeks more experience to feed the cosmic intelligence, you experience life where things attract and repel you. Things please you, scare you, anger you, sooth you, entwine you, ensnare you, baffle you, teach you, drip wisdom into you.

Why do we suffer?

Nothing teaches like pain and failure. Nothing.

Is it actually pain? I think so. I despised almost every lesson I've received and I can become physically sick when I contemplate some of the lessons I've experienced. Some of the pain accompanying those experiences has never left me, and I am a weaker individual because of the experience.

There is a cliché in our culture: 'That which does not kill you makes you stronger'. I find that cliché a lie, perpetuated to appease those suffering through intolerable experiences. What I have found is: That which almost kills me – *almost killed me*, and some of the wounds have not healed and I am worse for wear and worse from the experience. (just a personal perspective)

A quick anecdote regarding experience:

My father lost his battle with cancer when I was a teenager. He had been battling a few years when, during a specific casual moment alone, I said to him, "I can feel what you're going through." I loved him and felt the hurt of his pain and the fear of his uncertainty. But he gave me a lesson I have not forgotten. He responded, "Why? Do you have cancer?" I stood with my mouth open, and learned.

What does the Bible say regarding higher learning experiences?

Proverbs 3 **Wisdom Bestows Well-Being**

(But not like you think. Note: The ancient authors and their tribe weren't able to comprehend the concept of actual *spiritual existence* or *forgiveness*. The well-being referred to is: Spiritual well-being. The ancient authors had less awareness than we credit them.)

³ Let love and faithfulness never leave you; bind them around your neck, write them on the tablet of your heart.

¹¹ My son, do not despise the LORD's discipline, and do not resent his rebuke, ¹² because the LORD disciplines those He loves, as a father the son he delights in.

(Again – a rather impersonal teaching experience is misinterpreted as a personal admonition. The original author tribes twisted this perspective wrongly ...continually.)

¹³ Blessed are those who find wisdom, those who gain understanding, ¹⁴ for wisdom is more profitable than silver and yields better returns than gold. ¹⁵ She is more precious than rubies; nothing you desire can compare with her. ¹⁶ *Long life is in her right hand; in her left hand are riches and honor.*

(**Spiritual* long life. *Spiritual* riches and honor. Physical reward for doing what is right, doesn't exist. It is described in the Bible as 'vanity' ...fleeting ...temporary. God doesn't operate in fleeting temporary ways. This has been explained countless times, yet there are those insisting the gain is here in the physical. I'm sorry to be the next person in a countless procession to say; it is not.)

[18] She is a tree of life to those who take hold of her; those who hold her fast will be blessed.

(Not here, not temporary as is this life. Physical life isn't easier because we seek or find wisdom. The discovery process involves pain.)

[19] By wisdom the LORD laid the earth's foundations, by understanding he set the heavens in place; [20] by his knowledge the watery depths were divided, and the clouds let drop the dew.

(Please don't think God was this hands-on during the creation. He laid building-blocks we're just beginning to understand, and the biblical authors did not understand.)

[21] My son, do not let wisdom and understanding out of your sight, preserve sound judgment and discretion; [22] they will be life for you, an ornament to grace your neck.

You'll notice numbers missing. Yes. On purpose. Because wisdom doesn't help you walk straight, keep you upright, stop you from tripping, extend your life, or fill your silo with grain. Those concepts have nothing to do with the actual spiritual message, or the benefit to you. Those concepts are temporary and show exactly, the time and place factors the authors of that time and place were mired in. Wisdom helps your immortal being step an inkling closer to the most wonderful Being you can imagine. In the long run, that's worth far more than a large pile of wheat, or even gold that lasts only a single short lifetime.

Proverbs 4: 7

⁷Wisdom is supreme; therefor get **wisdom**. Though it cost all you have, get understanding. Getting **wisdom** is the wisest thing you can do!

Proverbs 8: 11

¹¹for wisdom is more precious than rubies, and nothing you desire can compare with her.

Proverbs 16: 16

¹⁶How much better to get wisdom than gold, to get insight rather than silver!

James 3: 17

¹⁷But the wisdom that comes from heaven is first of all pure; then peace-loving, considerate, submissive, full of mercy and good fruit, impartial and sincere.

(It's amazing how everything which is truly God and from God has the same gentle, loving, forgiving, perfection)

Nothing is as strong as gentleness; nothing so gentile as real strength. – St. Francis de Sales

*Would I trade my lessons now?* At least half. Some of them really sucked! I could have gone through this specific journey a little fatter, dumber, and happier. But I didn't seem to have a vote.

In seriousness, when I'm strong, I'm grateful for my lessons, but often I'm not strong. And when I'm not, my lessons weigh heavy on my heart, mind, and soul.

The parts of the Bible that tell us how much we gain in this life by being religious, or having wisdom, honor, etcetera; all the advantage promised - are all not accurate by my observation or experience. We gain no physical edge by being decent. If anything we're at a disadvantage. The spiritual advantage has nothing to do with any physical advantage, and this concept isn't new. It's written in the Bible, in James.

Doing right physically or spiritually doesn't benefit during this lifetime. It doesn't serve physical existence. It serves immortal existence. Believing so, aligns with the concept of a Perfect Immortal God.

There is something my defeat and failure have shown me: If you've had great success and think you have strong beliefs …let's just say, my earthly perspective has taught me enough to hope you don't get tested. My physical being knows what the tests taste like. I know the difference between having success and faith and having hardship and faith.

Success teaches almost nothing. Success doesn't strengthen you in any way. And failure tests your heart, mind, and soul, but shares lessons you can't afford no matter how successful you are.

And if the reason for existence is to learn, and become a better immortal being, then don't regret your failures and tests. There is good in everything we feel is bad and bad in everything we feel is good. Nothing good here is only good. Nothing bad here is only bad. The ancient symbol is ancient for a reason.

**The Meaning of Life**

How many noticed I described the meaning of life in the last section? The great question the sages of time couldn't answer (or have answered countless times, but the average human never understood). If you didn't notice, it may be because it's too simple, though that's God's calling-card.

I'll put it in a sentence:

The meaning of life is to experience all the experiences of mortal existence, which will teach our immortal being enough to someday allow us to enjoy the desired realm of spiritual existence, and commune with the spirits we all desire knowing.

How wonderful it would be to experience so much, we know love and forgiveness on the highest level, and our future existence experience is to help other beings learn and grow; loving and walking them through the process of experiencing, until they join us. To love them purely as we take them through their lessons. To forgive and love them as they curse us for the things not so pleasant, we must show them, so they too can comprehend all existence.

Because you cannot know the difference between fat and thin, if you're only fat OR thin. You cannot know what it feels like to be male and female if you're only male OR female. Rich-poor. Black-white. Healthy-sick…

Many people inaccurately believe, the people living through Biblical times knew what we know. This is called ethnocentrism: assuming the world has always existed from a current perspective. But people living two thousand years ago had no physical evidence of the cosmos. To assume they understood what we understand, or who God is, would be incorrect. They were busy getting run over by every titan king in walking distance. They didn't know their universe. They didn't know where the sun went at night. Seriously, they thought angels put it away at night but they didn't know where, and brought it out and raised it every morning.

…And evangelicals will say, 'They meant it metaphorically.'
No, they didn't.
These ancient people panicked when the winter solstice approached. They thought the sun was being put away as if by edict

from some bastard god they had failed to cower to properly. Not enough 'blood' sacrificed. Not enough young humans sacrificed.

The primary celebration was December twenty-fifth. (It's why Christmas is December twenty-fifth.) By the third day after the solstice, they saw the sun's daily time in the sky increasing again …and celebrated. Constantine changed the celebration of Ra (the sun god) to the celebration of his new God, when he became Christian.

'Keep Christ in Christmas' just shows a lack of complete knowledge, but the sentiment is appreciated.

Christ wasn't born on Christmas, and the Julian calendar miscalculates Christ's birth year. The renaissance monk who calculated got close, but missed. He didn't have the tools we now have. Humans recalculated using more modern instruments, and found his mistake, but it was too late to correct to the actual year.

There is roughly four billion years difference between the calendar year and the actual time of Earth's existence. Time of man is off by roughly a half million years. Scientists can run the genetic human chromosome code in reverse and identify a rough estimate of origin. The rough estimate is conservatively between 400,000 and 800,000 years, and the more calculations humans learn, the more science believes our existence may be on the other side of the larger number.

And whether the creationist religious like it or not, scientists can measure the age of our universe with impressive accuracy, and the age of any star including our sun, using molecular constants. The nuclear fusion process in a star is measurable and constant. We know a star's age by the percentages of helium and hydrogen. No creationist has to like it. It is what it is.

And the actual and natural occurrence of events can easily co-exist with a spiritual realm. The two ideas aren't mutually exclusive just like science and faith aren't mutually exclusive. In fact, quantum physics verifies the possibility of other universes.

And creationists: Your latest twist on the six day creation theory still has flaws. Do you know, if you study astronomy you'll learn the universe is *still* being created? I feel your pain. It's hard keeping a story pure when you start with antiquated inaccuracies as your foundation.

Wise men accept new information, and adjust paradigms accordingly. There is always new information to add to our current suppositions, and when new evidence is added, conclusions should adjust sequentially.

PS: Heaven isn't coming to this insignificant unimpressive ball of rock in this solar system, in this corner of this universe. Heaven is the founding universe of all creation and feeds all other universes. God isn't coming here or ending up here. We're going there and ending up there. We need to stop thinking so highly of ourselves that we think we're the center of anything. We're not, and the concept shows our cosmic infancy.

# Chapter Ten
## Bible Specifics

All aspects of the Ten Commandments are fascinating. First, how God is so hands on with these biblical tribes, but we haven't seen or heard from Him since. It is curious why only Moses ascended the mountain and was alone with God, and nobody questions his story.

'But Moses was the only human humble and pure enough to see God.' Think so? Read Leviticus. He's the supposed author.

The idea God interacted with us before humans could verify, is a topic for another lengthy discussion. It is curious why certain humans are supposedly in possession of the only proof God exists, yet leave it buried in a vault in Ethiopia and refuse to reveal it, when the organization likes displaying their religious artifacts more than anything they own. Why do they refuse to reveal this relic and end all doubt God exists, when they eagerly reveal far less impressive relics?

I've mentioned the governance hierarchy in the spiritual world, that rivals any major earth government, but am curious why the bible states, God took the time to come and visit in person ...and share explicit directions …as many concerning oxen, as humans. It must have been a Saturday …the Sabbath …God's original day off.

Psychology teaches, if humans can prove their point, beyond doubt, without cost, they gladly and immediately offer proof. Psychology also believes the opposite true.

If this religious organization had this relic, it would be sitting on the largest, highest, most expensive monument known to man, so this organization could gloat over all mankind. And this is a current day belief. Seven hundred years ago, when their religious leaders were ruling emperors, there's no doubt they would have lorded this celestial crowning jewel over the entire planet (forgive the pun).

Only ancient middle-easterners buried gold but this relic is so much more than gold. This relic would rule all religion, and due to our less than secular tendencies …the world. The additional set of 'commandments' I'll share, also could possibly make the religion owning the Ark, less than comfortable revealing their version of the *actual ten* commandments.

While examining the ten commandments, one day I noticed there's a commandment unlike all others. I referenced all gospel teaching, regarding this command and found, Christ spoke directly against this commandment. The lines are already referenced in this book. Christ's direct admonishment against everyone obeying this command.

Then I referenced the fourteen recently discovered commandments and noticed this commandment is missing. Nowhere to be even remotely misinterpreted to mean anything like this single command. It is not wise. It offers no profound sense of truth. It's the only command that doesn't serve humans. It's the only command that serves religion.

**The Ten Commandments**

Exodus 20:
20 "And God spoke all these words:
²I am the Lord your God, who brought you out of Egypt, out of the land of slavery."
³ "You shall have no other gods before me." -

But many civilizations have other gods and suffer no consequences. In fact, all of Israel's conquerors had *every* other god before this god, and one could argue, if gods have anything to do with nations conquering or being conquered, those gods defeated the ancient Israeli god, in almost every confrontation. Or could the Israeli god have won every conflict and He just let His people get annihilated on a regular basis. Or is God less 'hands-on' than the stories declare?

Does God just hate His chosen? Did He forget about the rest of the world or didn't the ancient middle-eastern tribes realize there's more to the world, and more people in the world, than they were aware?

⁴ "You shall not make for yourself an image in the form of anything in heaven above or on the earth beneath or in the waters below. ⁵ You shall not bow down to them or worship them; for I, the LORD your God, am a jealous God, punishing the children for the sin of the parents to the third and fourth generation of those who hate me, ⁶ but showing love to a thousand generations of those who love me and keep my commandments." -

If God punishes children for the sins of their parents, to the FOURTH generation – we're children of a disappointing god. If it matters whether you love or hate him ….it's better to not know him.

⁷ "You shall not misuse the name of the LORD your God, for the LORD will not hold anyone guiltless who misuses his name."

We don't **know** God's name. He refused to give it. Did God forget, or are the authors 'pretenders'? If you think God the Creator's name is Yahweh …**read something.** (hint: His name isn't Yahweh. That's the pronunciation twist humans gave the four unpronounceable consonants God gave us when we allegedly asked God Her name.) 'God Damn' means NOTHING. His name isn't *GOD*. Christ's name wasn't Jesus Christ. That was the Greek/Roman title given Him.

[8] "Remember the Sabbath day by keeping it holy. [9] Six days you shall labor and do all your work, [10] but the seventh day is a sabbath to the LORD your God. On it you shall not do any work, neither you, nor your son or daughter, nor your male or female servant, nor your animals, nor any foreigner residing in your towns. [11] For in six days the LORD made the heavens and the earth, the sea, and all that is in them, but he rested on the seventh day. Therefore the LORD blessed the Sabbath day and made it holy." -

The idea of a 6 *day* creation shows a human perspective based on authorship time and place. The creation is discussed in detail. Saturday is the 7th day of the week – not Sunday (1st day). The 'no work' idea is an antiquated concept which modern day humans have completely abandoned, and biblical humans abused. The Sadducees used this 'Commandment' to punish 'sinners' and it is supposedly the specific 'sin' Christ committed and was crucified for: healing a blind man on the Sabbath.

[12] "Honor your father and your mother, so that you may live long in the land the LORD your God is giving you." -

It is curious why spiritual commands for this group translate solely to physical benefits. Why this tribe has requisites for its land, and the rest of the world just lives without terms, is also curious. This tribe's god seems to be more merit oriented than all other 'false' gods, the other nations worship. Or is this list…embellished?

[13] "You shall not kill."
(actual translation: You shall not murder)
[14] "You shall not commit adultery."
[15] "You shall not steal."
[16] "You shall not give false testimony against your neighbor."
[17] "You shall not covet your neighbor's house. You shall not covet your neighbor's wife, or his male or female servant, his ox or donkey, or anything that belongs to your neighbor."

We'll ignore -for now- the idea God just directly condoned slavery in the tenth commandment, verse seventeen, in order to continue the primary discussion…

Synopsis

1. You shall have no other gods before Me.
2. You shall not make idols.
3. You shall not take the name of the LORD your God in vain.
4. Keep holy the Sabbath.
5. Honor your father and your mother.
6. You shall not murder.
7. You shall not commit adultery.
8. You shall not steal.
9. You shall not bear false witness against your neighbor.
10. You shall not covet.

Here are the commandments from a Dead Sea scroll that was blown up in Lebanon in the late nineteen hundreds as it was being prepared for introduction to the world:

Honor GOD as your king of wisdom
Treat others as you want to be treated
Respect those who teach and guide you
Do not kill except in self defense
Do not abuse power to exploit others
Refrain from greed
Refrain from envy
Be honest and true

Do not malign

Judge not falsely

Be no hypocrite

Know your worth

Wise use of resources

Help those in need

The other amazing aspect of this scroll is, non-religious humans claim they were led to it by non-human 'beings'. They were led directly to it, and the entire interaction and quest was documented. I once had internet access to the story. I can no longer find the information through either the old links or any browser search.

Please note: The where, when, and physical/historical context surrounding the scroll's discovery, indicate it was from the same place and time of origin as other religious scrolls, and this portends both the positive and negative time and place connotations and perspectives, all similar documents represent. But since it was unregulated and autonomous from the time written, to discovery, I find the content highly interesting.

1. This new commandments list seems unencumbered by years of possible human manipulation.

2. It fits more in-line with a Perfect Entity and His perfect maxims for Her children.

3.   It exposes the possibility, our existing commandments have been humanly manipulated enough to offer a more human, and thus, more flawed interpretation of spiritual edicts.

4.   It exposes a single original commandment as 'questionable'.

Point 4: The second list offers no reference to commandments that do not serve humanity, but these alternate commandments expose a peculiar discrepancy between the two lists: A single peculiar original commandment seems to serve a specific socio-political organization, which happens to not only be the institution which created and controlled the book these commandments are found in, but the supposed commandment is also contrary to the teachings of the Being the New testament swears it represents:

Christ specifically explained his disdain for those who worship in groups with public exposure and this disdain is not only found in the Bible, it is found in what is considered one of the four most revered books in the Bible – the Gospel. It is not only a prevalent Gospel excerpt, it is considered the most intricate and lengthy teaching Christ offered humans - The Sermon on the Mount – in the Gospel of Matthew. – (Mat 5-7)

The specific referenced commandment: Keep holy the Sabbath.

This commandment not only has nothing in common with the other commandments on either list, but also seems to only serve the entity parenting its existence. It is also contrary to the teachings of the God, from which Christian religious organizations exist.

And the only way to counteract inaccurate human paradigms is to decertify, then expose them.

In the Christian realm, the commandment: *Keep holy the Sabbath*, is connoted as church worship. As mentioned before, Christ spoke specifically against church worship in the Sermon on the Mount. – Matthew 6: 5-8

(NOTE: 'Synagogue' is an untranslated word. It is one of the very few untranslated words in the bible. It's translation is 'church'. All other words in that excerpt and that thought have been translated. That word too, needs translating, to understand and adhere to the Christ's instruction. You can surmise why it is untranslated.)

Why then do formal Christian organizations promote church worship? Might it have something to do with human motives and concerns?

You don't have to look hard or long to discover other similarities between today's religious organizations and the Sadducees of Christ's time. It takes almost no effort to measure the similar anti-Christ messages of both. Neither held or holds love over law. Neither welcomed or welcomes all. Both were/are extremely ritualistic – when Christ spoke against rituals.

The Sabbath commandment does not serve God or Her children. It serves only religion. But if you have a need or desire to follow religious mandate, instead of the Being the religion holds as its foundation and God, please feel free to continue.

Many are uncomfortable opening the Bible. Many read the Bible with dread, afraid to discover yet another action they can't do or way they're going to fail to please God or reach heaven.

This may be why religious people don't read the Bible. God, through Bible authors, talks about *love* being the most important aspect of existence, and in the next Bible passage, God is depicted as a brutal heartless bastard…an ornery unforgiving overbearing ogre. (God is NOT.)

Look at the two sets of commandments again (measuring the first in its textual setting). Could the Creator God of the Bible be any more overbearing and sociopathic in His approach? Yet He wants us to be *nothing but* meek in temperament, forgiving and loving in nature?

And the second list. Does the second list seem less overbearing? Does it seem less ramification-oriented? There are no earthly penalties or rewards mentioned.

Does the overbearing approach lead to a higher percentage or a more devoted following? Christ didn't use the overbearing sociopathic approach as He won disciples. He asked us to love like He loved us.

It's curious to note that as Christianity was established, *overbearing* became the organization's primary characteristic. Could this dogmatic approach to the desire for religious conformity have influenced the overbearing undertone and misinterpretation of the original commandments, and other bible messages?

Our religious organizations look amazingly like the Sadducees; the pretend religious Christ spoke against. Humans seem to repeat actions as if we were in a continual loop.

Do we have the ability to break the loop? Knowledge may be the crack in the loop. My knowledge starts with observation. I let no one convince me to believe them, instead of my 'lying' eyes. Feel free to adopt the mindset.

**The Tenth Commandment**

You didn't think I was not going to address the condonation of slavery in the bible, did you?

Exodus 20
[20] And God spoke all these words:

20:17You shall not covet your neighbor's house. You shall not covet your neighbor's wife, **or his male or female servant**...

... "And **GOD** spoke these words"? God condones slavery?

Male or female servant? Servant as in *slave*? ...God's own words?

Some people can't find a flaw in the bible. Does that mean they believe in slavery? (Not owning one – BEING ONE!)

Dear religion,

Please dig up the ten commandments and show the world whether or not God condones slavery.

Other bible verses which explain *How to treat your slaves* are mentioned in this document. For those who accept the words, verbatim: No, God doesn't condone slavery, and the human author was mired in his time and place.

20And God spoke all these words...

...probably not.

I wrote this section, and put the manuscript away. I don't want to write that the Bible or our most revered religions have no idea who God is, and writing it makes me uncomfortable. The exercise is me fighting all the paradigms drilled into my being since I was old enough to comprehend communication.

I decided last night that I can't write this book. I promised I wouldn't throw it away, but decided I would stop indefinitely, and went to bed thinking, God doesn't need me to explain who He is. God is God. She can do anything She wants. She creates UNIVERSES, and I'm a cosmic newborn from the corner of existence. Who the fuck am I to write who God is?

I thought as I lie in bed, I'll calm my words. I'll take the edge off my thoughts. I can write with an edge, especially things I'm passionate about, and I'm passionate about the God I was reintroduced to. I'm passionate about the discrepancy between the true nature of God and the antiquated inaccurate definition humans are currently using.

I seem to see a naiveté in certain human beliefs, and believe the people who are sharing these antiquated paradigms should know better, but they're having physical success preaching these inaccurate paradigms. Circumstantial success has given them the pulpit, and positive physical reinforcement has solidified their inaccurate antiquated mindset. And I get demoralized when they preach things they know less about, than they realize. Nationwide surveys show most preachers receive the same test grades as do atheists, when taking Bible question tests.

I know I can have this edge. I've tried to quell this edge throughout this project and my life, and it's hard. I feel like yelling *STOP HURTING PEOPLE WITH YOUR CHILDISH BELIEFS!*

I think to myself: Instead, be your Father's child! He is pure perfect love. Stop railing! All I'm doing is offending the people I'm trying to tell how wonderful God is! And then it struck me how God is perfect, but I'm *not*. How *hard* it is to be like God and how easy it is to fall into human traps and human idiosyncrasies. I'm *human*. Do I want to love like God tells me I need to love? I want nothing more. Nothing.

I fail – and in many aspects, so did the original Bible writers. Not on purpose. They were just like me. They were being who they are, during the time they existed.

But in many other instances, they succeeded! They went beyond success! Many were able to go stretches of writing, explaining their concepts of a Perfect God and His perfect love.

Their stories about God were just from their perspective …and that's completely acceptable. What has become unacceptable is: we stopped understanding the stories *are* only from their perspective and *are* limited by their time and place of existence.

Humans fail. I fail. And any word or sentence you read in this document, that seems harsh or demeaning, please understand it is <u>me</u> who fails you, and not God. I fail horribly …hourly. It's what I do best. Religion fails next.

God fails at nothing. God fails you – never.

I'm a failure at everything I've ever attempted, while receiving visits from beings that scare the shit out of me. My life is cursed, and I'm exhausted.

But the curse has led to this work, as if all my failures have left me with nothing, but to do this project.

I prayed last night asking if I could be done this project. I asked for help with taking the demeaning edge off my words. And was told, keep writing.

But I'm reluctant. This is already my life:

James 3: [3]Not many of you should become teachers, my brothers, for you know that we who teach will be judged with greater strictness.

~~~

There are three commands on the Bible list that aren't on the list blown up in Lebanon. All three are early century middle-east culture influenced. The middle-east people seem to have a raw passion, other parts of the world have learned to quell, and parts of the Bible represent that raw edge.

I've come to learn, God doesn't have that raw edge. Think about it. Nothing that old which has seen that much existence has that raw edge. Nothing that is perfect love has that raw edge.

Nothing about forgiving has that raw edge. You cannot cut yourself or others on *love* and *forgive*.

### The Ark of the Covenant

If an organization had the real Ark of the Covenant and it had the commandments they say it has, the Ark would adorn the greatest monument known to man. If the commandment list was manipulated to serve the religious organization controlling the words in the Bible, and commands in the bible were adjusted to suit a more selfish purpose, maybe a religion would want to keep it buried somewhere. But if it has what they say, I can't comprehend them insisting it remain buried.

The organization wants everyone to be Christian, don't they? The Ark would guarantee it, wouldn't it? The organization has to know that, don't they? But the organization still doesn't know women are equal to men in God's eyes, nor do they accept lgbt. They don't even accept other religions worshipping the same God.

I've measured these organizations, and from their declining enrollment, I'm deducing others are measuring them also. May I suggest, their unbending inclination to hold steadfast to unfounded antiquated paradigms may be the cause? These organizations refuse to acknowledge the inconsistencies being discovered in many aspects of their founding stories.

Is this refusal the reason supporting the current spiritual tension? Existence is showing signs, humans are ready to move forward, and religion's insistence humans not move forward in their universal development, may indicate a forthcoming breaking point. Will this development be quick? Humanly noticeable? God seems to work on a protracted timeline, but birth-pains are emerging.

**How many Religious Commandments?**
**The Ten (Fourteen) versus Hundreds of Commandments**

God gave us ten or fourteen commandments (or rules). Religions' commandments (or rules) are often in the hundreds. Are you aware of the extra almost countless rules?

In one religion, there are seven 'sacraments', considered by their organization to be as adherent-worthy as the ten/fourteen commands God supposedly insists we honor.

Some say, all the rules in the Bible are of equal merit, because they came from humans with God-given exception transcending time and place. I've proven that inaccuracy. And with the refuting of validity, offer an observation:

There are two levels of command in the Bible.
1. God's – At least for the rules that sound like God may have given them. They're not hard to honor. (I choose to believe the fourteen sound like the God I've come to

believe in.) I also choose to recognize Christ's additional command as a commanded rule, out of admiration for Him, and the purity of the request. John 13: 34-35. It is too perfect not to respect the rule and the author.
2. Human – The remaining religious rules aren't rules to be concerned with, but if you disagree, understand: You can hold to, or make extra commandments for yourself, but I advise avoiding this practice. It is written: you will be held to your additional commandments.

And whether you do or don't hold yourself to the additional rules, hurting others by holding your additional commandments against others, is a practice worthy of God's enemy.

[14]I know and am convinced in the Lord Jesus that nothing is unclean in itself; but to him who thinks anything to be unclean, to him it is unclean. Romans 14:14

(This passage legitimizes LGBT too. Isn't it peculiar how the pure passages all align with the concept of a *perfect* God?)

But there is a flaw exposed in this beautiful passage, when society's influence on each individual is contemplated.

What happens when the individual is repeatedly bullied into believing their inner nature is unclean, when they know in their heart it isn't? Does God then hold that individual to the perspective she or he now has due to the constant bombardment of inaccuracy? (the insisted-upon immature social paradigm supporting the misconception)

Even the most beautiful human perspectives can show human shortsightedness.

Dear brother and sister: Your Measurer is Perfect. You are exonerated when your crime is: being bullied into believing inaccuracies. It is your bully, who will receive lessons, accordingly.

# Chapter Eleven
## The Eradication of Hell

### Hell vs A Perfect Loving God

Every religion has a 'hell'. There is no reason to believe there's no such place. From what I've experienced, this wonderful ball of rock we currently occupy, fits all the criteria of hell, and the concept is shared at the end of this discussion, but for now, I'll try to keep the argument to fairly objective mental and spiritual aspects of human existence.

The Christian definition of 'hell' and eternal damnation for failing in our game of hide-n-seek with an ancient venomous god, is explicitly unique to the Christian organization. In fact, it positively correlates with the definition of psychopathic. Some fine and impressive humans, without visiting this unique location (there is no supposed exit), decided there is a special putrid eternal place for all humans failing their departure requisites, including ones who die at birth—which is the epitome of the most fucked up cruelty man or cosmic being can conceive? ... And this is the entity we need to kneel to every seventh day (or 'period of time')?

And *after* this being curses me (to the 4th generation) for things my mother and father, grandmothers and grandfathers, and grandmothers' and grandfathers' mothers and fathers did, I get to spend eternity in a pool of flaming vomit under eternal torture, for nothing more than being born?

But wait. I didn't ask to be born. Am I to believe, I didn't exist, and then my mother and father decided to love a baby, so they had me, and because we don't believe in this religion, I'm doomed to spend eternity in perpetual torment?

If some fine human tells you this is who your God is, please consider running from them screaming, after memorizing her or his face, so you can warn others what this demon-like earth-creature looks like.

At best, hell is a place God has supposedly designated for spiritual beings who opposed Him during their attempt to overthrow him. I personally don't know the story firsthand, nor do I care. That seems to be between God and some of his spiritual subjects. But even though I don't have information to verify or refute the story, I can identify discrepancies in it.

First, there is supposedly no creature in existence, God didn't create, so who is God's equal? Why would these inferior beings then feel they had the power to forcefully oppose their creator? Why would they care to oppose their creator? What is their creator doing that would conjure the need to consider such a radical response?

Humans are often ruled by people posing as lower lifeforms, but rarely do we act physically against them. Only after all other less radical alternatives are exhausted, is this last desperate radical option considered, let alone enacted. If you go back to the *original* creation story predating the current Bible story, God fought a water creature, who by description of the battle, held its own before succumbing, so maybe there are creatures that exist whom God didn't create …**or**

**…or…**

**or**…humans like telling stories, some of which were accidentally accepted as truth …or… humans are unfathomably more clueless than we imagine ourselves.

'But our current explanation of hell is real!'

Prove it. Authenticate its origins and existence. Show its credentials. Give reasons. Verify. No assumptions. No exceptions.

I would also like to question who told this story to whom, in order for it to get handed down far enough to finally be included in our human truths, our sacred religious text.

The oldest current story of this advocate (Satan) is in the book of Job. The Bible's book of Job is also not original. The story has many older versions throughout the history of the Middle East, but they all have the advocate (Satan) participating in a docile, if not pleasant meeting with God the Creator. The human named Job comes up in conversation, and when God mentions how Job is a good 'servant', the advocate explains, it is due to the earthly gifts God has bestowed on Job. The story explains, God acknowledges Satan's argument and decides to 'test' Job's servitude and loyalty by allowing Satan to torture him, to see if Job remained as faithful and loyal.

God's and Satan's uncaring heartless cruelty in the story is a topic for a different conversation, but the point is, God and Satan look nothing like warring factions in the story. Satan as the story is told, was not God's enemy. He was an advocate for the opposing opinion in nothing more than a judicial spiritual discussion.

Non-modern humans saw God as the ultimate judge, and imagined Him spending His existence judging everyone. Lord knows there are humans who spend their entire waking life judging others, so I can envision certain humans thinking this must be what God does His entire existence. What a strangely boring activity for such an advanced ancient Being.

Remember, the Job story predates all other stories regarding Satan, and Satan and hell seem to grow in anti-godlike strength and attitude throughout Christianity's evolution. Humans seem to need a villain equally opposing a good hero, for their best tales. The current Satan's anger and strength make the best tale. There's even an epic battle planned, for the conclusion – again…as if Satan is God's equal and can display equal power and authority against God.

So God supposedly made this place He imprisons opposing angels for a thousand years at a time, though I have no proof. The story says God also lets them out every thousand years, though I'm confused why God would use the orbit of this nondescript planet as a time guideline for something in the spiritual universe, but let's go with it…

During their hiatus from their thousand year imprisonment, these God-opposing angels supposedly come to Earth and torture us.

Do I believe children of God can join this anti-God faction, or go to hell at any point in their existence? I'm more inclined to believe in a spiritual death (the second death spoken of) than I am an eternal damnation. Eternal damnation is a little too close to psychopathically extreme, even for the ancient middle-easterners' and early Christians' god.

Do I have reasons to believe there may be a sanction of beings who oppose God, and attempt to act in opposition to His wishes? My experiences can be viewed in a perspective which would lend credence to the idea, though with greater contemplation, I'm more inclined to believe *all* difficulties we encounter are instead nothing more than learning experiences, even if they include what look like spiteful acts of unfriendly spiritual beings.

Have I witnessed unexplained spiritual activity I can argue is outside any 'learning' experience, which supports the former above argument? Yes.

Will I share my thoughts regarding that opinion? No, except to say: When you're allowed to view even the edges of the spiritual universe, and you stare into the abyss, it not only stares back, but you also see things which aren't understood or explained.

Will I share more explicit detail? No, because if you haven't lived the experience, understanding it is impossible. I don't understand things I've experienced, that pertain to outside what the typical person would describe as the normal parameters of our physical universe. Thinking others could understand without the experience is something psychology teaches is impossible.

Is this situation worthy of concern? No. This situation seems to be between occupants of the spiritual universe, and though I've seen glimpses of confusing interaction, God has full control over the level of harm that can befall Her children (us), which means, even the actions which seem like nothing more than spiritual spite, are still nothing but lessons.

The idea hell is for humans, diametrically opposes everything my argument offers. It diametrically opposes everything I've been taught and everything I've experienced. Does hell exist? The answer doesn't matter to humans. We were told by angels, we are held above certain spiritual beings, including angels. With that supposition, I can surmise, maybe certain parameters certain beings are held to, do not affect all beings equally. With greater knowledge and awareness, might come greater expectations for self-control, and subsequently greater admonishment for failure, but I have no proof of such action.

The spiritual universe exists. We, the children of God, in all our manifestations across this and all other universes, become blissful visitors to the spiritual realm, between non-spiritual existences. The continual spiritual stop-over is based on the ideas: We exist to learn. God makes nothing temporary. Our spiritual beings are immortal. God is Love/Forgive. We are God's children. We're who He loves/forgives, and teaches. And… God is *perfect*.

I am also led to believe there is also a growth in this ongoing spiritual visitation, where more of the spiritual universe is revealed as our abilities to accept new revelations grow. And this idea leads me to believe there are more fascinating existences to experience, than we currently comprehend.

Where did the Christian concept of hell come from?

The fledgling Christian religion passed through Greece when that society believed in Greek Mythology. Cultures, especially well-established cultures, don't just throw away current beliefs when new ideas are presented. The new ideas are interwoven into the existing belief system.

The radical idea of Christianity to those believing in Greek mythology, is similar to the radical ideas in this book and how they will be considered by those believing in the current version of Christianity. Some will embrace the new concepts. Some will reject them wholeheartedly. Some will attempt to find a happy medium by melding the ideas. And there is no way to foretell what the final acceptance paradigms will be.

The stories of hell in Greek society and mythology are supported by their caves of fire, they proudly profess as the entrance(s) to hell. Greece is built on ancient volcanos, with many visible 'hotspots' considered gateways to hell and the underworld. Caves and holes where 'hell' can not only be seen, but stand close enough and you can feel the heat. It's as hot as hell. (pun intended)

Can I find any verification validating the putrid psychopathological argument non-conforming humans go to a place of eternal timeless torture, and are sent there by a loving wonderful perfect God? Do I need to validate the preposterousness of that concept with an answer?

Satan was nothing more than an advocate before Christianity was founded. All he did was make the argument humans aren't worthy of God's love or forgiveness. Our problem with Satan: Our counter argument doesn't exist. Humans continue to abuse everything we encounter. We abuse each other. We abuse our earth. We're starting to abuse the space around our earth. Humans make no counter-argument, we're worthy of God's love.

We humans like to profess we're some higher life-form, closer to God in all aspects of experiential existence, but our actions and mindset still prove we're cosmic children. When do we start showing God we're growing up?

Certain stories have no validity except they're untraceably old. There are countless fairytales, myths, and legends. I'm not saying none are true. Believe what you need to believe. Even feel free not to question some of the bullshit. Just please be kind enough to refrain from sharing unquestioned unverified bullshit with innocent others. We're doing more harm to our next generations than we realize.

The idea - Earth is Hell:

A well-established ancient religion describes hell as: The place furthest from God. See Him anywhere?

I'd like to put this ancient unfounded idea of hell to bed. It's fucking ridiculous, and it's part of the reason some of our children are committing suicide at an alarming rate.

Dear religious: Your version of hell doesn't exist. Do you see the spiritual imperfection in the premise? And God is exactly the opposite.

Side note: The Pope was caught saying hell doesn't exist, then retracted the statement after his organization scolded him. It's alright Francis. We appreciate you trying to tell the world the truth. Work on your courage, dear friend.

**Bible Summation**

Parts of the Bible are wonderful. Parts express and share great love and wisdom. Other parts spew hate, animosity, and exclusion. These other parts feed the evil in this world, and allow it to not only exist, but also to thrive.

Please see the difference. Please, if you're not able to use original ways to separate the love and wisdom from the hate and childishness, please use Siddhartha Gautama's method of discernment:

"Do not believe in anything simply because you have heard it. Do not believe in anything simply because it is spoken and rumored by many. Do not believe in anything simply because it is taught... found written...or is tradition... But after observation and analysis, when you find that anything agrees with reason and is conducive to the good and benefit of one and all, then accept it and live up to it." – Siddhartha Gautama

Under the premise: If it looks like a duck, waddles like a duck, and quacks like a duck...it's probably a duck. If the bible's words sound childish, hurtful, and without love and wisdom; if honoring them would hurt brothers and sisters, they're probably not love and wisdom. And if that's the case, they don't represent a perfect loving, anciently old, wise God, and are okay to eliminate from our lives.

**The Sadducees vs Current Religions**

Religion and Christ were never closely connected. Christ often ridiculed, ignored, and defied the Sadducees, (the religious rulers and leaders of His time) as if their laws meant nothing. His teachings went against religious edict, and the Sadducees tried (and failed) to trip Christ regularly with religious based philosophical conundrums.

The Sadducees were scared of Christ. He continually called them out for their childish bullshit. (sound familiar?)

I've found many uncomfortable differences between Christ and the current Christian religions' teachings. Many of them have already been discussed. This is a discussion about the similarities between the Sadducees and current religious leadership…

Christ didn't come here to create a religion. His teachings were so different from the existing religious law ruling his culture, humans felt the need to found a new religion in His honor. Why then do certain current Christian religions look so similar to the Sadducees Christ opposed during His time teaching?

The Torah is considered the foundation of the religion considered the foundation of Christianity, but the concept of the Jewish religion being the foundation of Christianity, was argued during the creation of the formal Christian religion. The conclusion those humans adopted, to leave the two religions somewhat connected, was based more on geographical proximity and previous relationships of the new religion's authors, than any related content or contextual association. Those founding Christianity were afraid to completely throw away the old, which is typical, normal, and natural.

The New Testament tells Christians the old testament law has been voided. Why then have current religions readopted old testament laws?

Christ was tried for breaking a religious law, so He obviously had already broken from those antiquated beliefs of the founding religion. Transferring any of those original beliefs into the new religion, seems to go against the words and actions of the Christian religion's founding God.

The Christ spoke often and derogatorily about the religious authority which existed during His life on earth. He ignored, defied, and ostracized the Sadducees constantly, and for the few mentions in the Gospels, the stories make it clear, the Sadducees tried regularly to trip Christ spiritually, and wanted to remove Christ from their list of concerns.

His alleged fatal crime: He healed a blind man while traveling. He stopped as a poor blind soul asked Him for help, knowing He could cure, and Christ relented. It is believed, He supposedly mixed His saliva with the dusty dirt on the side of a road, and placed it on the blind person's eyes, curing him.

His crime? He did this on the Sabbath, and religious law of the time and place, forbade work on the Sabbath.

His actual crime? There obviously was none. In fact, Christ's action was nothing but love transcending His physical time and place. It was also an act against the religious childishness which existed during His time and place of physical existence.

Further similarities between the Sadducees and current religious organizations...

Christ destroyed Sadducee rituals, Christian religion reinstated rituals.

Christ welcomed all. He went out of His way to welcome those, the religious of His time excluded. Christian religions, like the Sadducee, refuse entire groups.

Christ treated all equal. Certain sects of Christianity from their inception to this day, don't recognize females or lgbt as equal.

Christ destroyed religious law. Religion has reinstated laws specifically against Christ's teachings.

Current Christian humans deciding to voluntarily imitate the Sadducees, instead of the Christ, when all their beliefs supposedly have Christ as their single primary foundation and focus, seems to have reverted many back to the mindset Christ tried with His life to move us beyond.

If Christians have as their singular primary religious focal point – the Christ, who destroyed all religious law and replaced it with love, then why have they adopted so little of Christ's teaching, and so *much* of the Sadducees religious immaturity, rituals, and childish laws? What happened?

No, I'm not asking as a precursor to sharing the answer with you. I'm asking because the entire two-thousand year loop back to the original problem of childish religious activity – confuses me. I feel like we're witnessing the empowerment of an organization called:

## Christians Against Christ

Christians who hate, judge, exclude …spend time in a building, mindlessly performing rituals Christ ostracized, while never focusing on the messages which explain Christ's new terms of human conduct?

Many of these peoples' ancestors were also highly religious. Many were highly religious slave-owners. Many are currently highly religious bigots.

Christians Against Christ. …amazing.

[6]Jesus answered them, "Isaiah prophesied correctly about you hypocrites, as it is written: 'These people honor Me with their lips, but their hearts are far from Me. [7]They worship in vain; they teach as doctrine the precepts of men.' [8]You have disregarded the commandment of God to keep the tradition of men."… Mark 7: 6-8

**Matthew 7:21-23 English Standard Version (ESV)**
**I Never Knew You**

[21] "Not everyone who says to me, 'Lord, Lord,' will enter the kingdom of heaven, but the one who does the will of my Father who is in heaven. [22] On that day many will say to me, 'Lord, Lord, did we not prophesy in your name, and cast out demons in your name, and do many mighty works in your name?' [23] And then will I declare to them, 'I never knew you; depart from me, you workers of lawlessness.'

If you wish to move from mindless pretend-Christian to actual Christ disciple (Christian) …Love. Forgive. Accept. Read, pray and evaluate privately. Contemplate Christ's teachings. May I suggest you start with the Bible quotes enclosed.

If you're already honoring your God with efforts toward love / forgiveness, and acceptance, even if you fail repeatedly, your brothers and sisters thank you.

~~~

Wisdom and understanding are a two-edged sword. You get to be aware of things others aren't, but you also get to be confused why others can't see what you see. –

**Religious Leaders:** Like God requests things of me, may I share a request with you:

Re-evaluate your message. If it is not one of unconditional love of a perfect perfect Being and inclusion without judgement, understand you are being asked to change your message. Your message is causing some of God's children to learn some less-than-Godly beliefs, and your actions do not serve our God or Her children, our brothers and sisters. Your message has been noticed.

Please be aware, your greatest concern will come to pass if corrections aren't made.

If your message is one of unconditional love/forgiveness, thank you for serving our brothers and sisters. Please continually emphasize and re-emphasize your teaching. Please be louder, more adamant, more persistent, and more vocal about your unconditional acceptance of all God's children, under the terms, God is perfect and makes no mistakes. All Her children are exactly what God made, therefore your opinion on their normality should come distantly after your trust in our God.

You must also be louder and more persistent than those offering opposing messages, ideas, and laws negatively affecting our brothers and sisters. Everyone is hearing the negative narrative. It's impossible to block out. Evolutionary psychology has proven, humans give even false negative messages of warning, much more credence than they give messages of safety and well-being. Heeding warning was necessary for survival for so long, it became an evolutionary instinct.

And your silence to the ungodly messages of some of your peers speaks volumes, and has been well heard. If it is unintentional, please correct.

Please add to your message, the idea you not only preach unconditional love and inclusion, but you also disagree with people who preach otherwise. Your flock is hearing other preacher's words, and though you're saying the right ones, they are hearing both right and wrong, and psychology teaches: If the wrong message is shared often and passionately, it can be adopted even with great trepidation.

There is a noticeable deviation by certain Christian organizations, from the puritan perspective. Some religious organizations are teaching and preaching more on the lines of love and acceptance, though with further examination, these organizations are still placing an unrealistic emphasis on some old testament Bible stories. I hope we can de-emphasize stories which show obvious spiritual and universal shortcomings …with the hope, progressive information and awareness will continue to help those trying to deviate from the antiquated fire and brimstone perspective.

There once was a great modern evangelical preacher who had such a large following, he was known world-wide. He traveled the world, preaching to large crowds …but no matter how much he preached and no matter how much he projected a spiritual connection, he refused to accept the LGBT community.

This would have been acceptable if he had given a reason, but he never did (I know it's because there isn't one – see the extensive argument below). To his dying day, all he would say about LGBT was: LGBT lifestyle is wrong.

He had a child, who uses the father's name to also preach, though the progeny's hate and anger come through more clearly. The progeny too insists LGBT is wrong, but in a more 'fire and brimstone' way. This person too never gives a reason, but is more adamant than the famous father; the unfounded religious righteousness so prevalent in this person, it exudes from the person's being.

This person has a podium, like the father had a podium, and pontificates with an amazing conviction, but never a reason.

"LGBT is wrong." They say.

I have no podium, famous name, or notoriety. I've only studied the subject…weighed its supposed crime…its supposed offense against God and nature.

So why do I have a completely different opinion on this subject? Why do I feel the LGBT lifestyles are as natural as any other expression of love, gender, or sex?

You would think it's because I studied the subject, but that's only the byproduct of the answer — the confirmation of the hypothesis. The motive which led to my study, then opinion, is based on one concept: The difference between what I've observed and what others would like me to believe: Deciding to think for myself, instead of mindlessly accepting the programming we're all processed through.

## Our Programming

"To repeat what others have said, requires education; to challenge it, requires brains." – Mary Pettibone Poole

We make the next generations of leaders by telling our children to sit down and shut up. It's brilliant. Brilliantly lazy, brilliantly mindless, brilliantly easy to conform to.

We're all programmed by our loved-ones and their assigned representatives (teachers). We're all programmed at too young an age to realize we're being programmed. No, it is not the paranoia programming horror movies are made of. It's 'good' programming. It teaches conformity. The programming allows us to conform to the accepted norms of our society, even when those norms oppose our accumulated wisdom.

It has one drawback though. We learn conformity by learning not to think. It's inferred, people before us already did the thinking, so it's reasonable to assume previous verification, isn't it?

An example of conformity without thought:

Equality – We not only believe 'all men are created equal', we proudly profess, it's one of our founding societal pillars.

Where do we find equality in our society?

In books. You won't find it anywhere else. It's not in our opinion of race, creed, ethnicity, color, gender, sexual preference, financial concern, education...anywhere. Our government won't sanction it. Our religions fear it. Our corporations ignore it. Financial equality is considered un-American. Equality is found nowhere but in books. We believe wholeheartedly in the concept. We love the wisdom. Practical application?

We believe in equality. Just ask any patriotic American. Then ask the person if her or his parents instilled the belief in them, or maybe it was a grade school teacher?

Our programming allows us to blend into our society and continue the beliefs of our parents, guardians and elders without questioning thought. It helped the great evangelical preacher's offspring perpetuate a heartfelt message ...no matter that neither ever studied the subject in order to build an intellectual foundation for their beliefs.

I examined my programming. Have you ever evaluated yours? Be careful. The associated revelations may scare the living shit out of you. I know when I began the process, I became terrified by my initial programming revelations, and I believe I was guided through the process. Attempting the process without guidance may be even more daunting.

An excerpt from a previous work:
[      I remember Catholic school teaching all the ways I can go to hell. Back then, masturbation was a big no-no to the nuns

who taught us. I wonder if they still give it the same emphasis. Anyway, lgbt was right up there on their list of 'guaranteed hell tickets' and in fact, they used to declare that you have a conscience and you know in your conscience that it's wrong. You can feel it and that's the holy spirit telling you.

Forty years later I learn, through child psychology, we're all born a blank slate. **'Tabula rasa'.** Feral child studies confirm this.

**Tabula rasa:** the epistemological idea that individuals are born without built-in mental content and therefore all knowledge comes from experience or perception. (see feral child studies)

Which is it? Do we have a built in conscience or not?

You're all aware of diapers. Does a baby have any inkling that pooping or peeing itself is something to be embarrassed about? How about walking around naked? Bathing? Sticking something …everything in their mouth …even disgusting things?

Everything you believe is either something you've figured out or something you've been taught …and almost all of what you've been taught, is something you were told to believe before you were old enough to stop the teacher and tell them, 'Hey wait a minute. That sounds like Bullshit.'

What percent of the nuns who teach grade school do you think have advanced psych degrees? Is there any reason for a 2$^{nd}$ or 3$^{rd}$ grader not to believe the Nun teacher or question her statements?

After all, they're gods, aren't they? No, wait. They're God's wife. They're 'married to God'. They wear wedding rings.

Contrary to what some of us were taught, everything you believe - you learned. It is why some people in other parts of the world believe things you don't and don't believe things you do.

Anyone fear the number 13? Anyone think it's cursed? Do you know the origin of western civilization's belief the number 13 is cursed? That's how many people were at the last supper dinner table, and one died almost immediately following. The problem is, there wasn't a dinner table. They ate reclining on the floor, and there weren't 13 people there. The famous Renaissance painting only shows 13 people.

In China, they fear the number 4. Anyone in western civilization not of Chinese descent fear the number 4? Have I convinced you yet that you've learned everything you believe? Studies show, our thought is language based and even language is something learned and not natural. And people of different languages think in different concepts. Don't believe it? Go on an international internet social media site and access a foreign account, then hit 'translate'. It isn't the failure of the translation program. Some languages do not translate well with each other. ]

We're politely programmed, which often includes suppressing independent thinking. Society feels better served by conformity, but history proves, innovative thought fuels human development. Society always benefits from advancement, and religion has fought human intellectual development from its inception.

Even though the information in this book may be unsettling, can you understand why it's necessary to re-evaluate things believed unquestioningly? Nothing stands against change, and intelligent change starts with assessment.

Younger people identify cultural inconsistencies better than older adults and are often more willing to enact change. Some are questioning adult paradigms and motives, and identified cultural incongruence is causing concern. I've had this discussion with an estimated three thousand adolescents, and a majority have confirmed.

May I suggest opening an intellectual dialog with the next generations. They'll be inheriting what we leave them. You'll be pleasantly surprised by how enlightening their perceptions are, regarding what we're leaving them.

Society honors its live conformists and its dead non-conformists. – Mignon McLaughlin

# Chapter Twelve
## The Argument for LGBT Normality

**– by the Learned, Including Christ - in His Own Words**

People who have never tasted something should not tell people who are eating, how they should react to the taste. –

This section is in defense of a specific group of humans currently being bullied. I'd like to apologize to the readers who are not part of this situation, but humbly ask you to continue reading so you may know the foundation behind your point of view, further understand the unfounded basis for this injustice, and possibly stand less quietly when in the company of those discussing this situation.

If you believe like I, that all humans are equal, and all humans deserve the freedoms many of us hold dear, yet everyone doesn't enjoy … if you believe our freedoms are the foundation of our existence, and rightfully ours for no other reason than we exist, then I humbly ask you to contemplate the next narrative.

Bullies look for, and often find weaker humans. Certain current bullies have found their latest weak group of humans, and the situation needs to be brought to light in greater detail than is currently being discussed. I'm not referring to individually weak humans. I'm referring to collectively weak. Weak as in, they're continually being denied equality, supposedly in the name of God.

The LGBT are currently considered less than equal. They are weaker politically. They're weaker religiously, for the incorrect reasons enclosed. They are lesser in number because those who openly identify are being ridiculed and threatened to the point of hiding to survive. They're not only denied basic rights of life the bullies enjoy and demand, but the children belonging to this group are four times more likely to commit suicide than children outside this group.

That last sentence is my main contention. – *FOUR TIMES* more likely to commit suicide…because there's a certain group telling them they're 'condemned to eternal hell', for no reason other than who they know they are. Fine humans are killing our children by telling them things they know nothing about, and this ongoing injustice needs addressing.

Majorities deny minorities equality. Males still refuse acknowledgement of female equality. Majority religious deny minority religions and non-religious. People refusing equality to brothers and sisters because of some and all perceived nonconformity. But the only current minority having their lives threateningly altered in all corners of the Earth is the minority based on sexual orientation and gender non-conformity.

Nothing is more offensive than our children deciding suicide is their only option, for the lack of love, support, and supporting argument they receive, and it is time to offer that supporting argument and reveal exactly how unfounded the opposing argument is.

The following is a previously written in-depth breakdown of the lack of foundation for one of the longest ongoing instances of bullying injustice known to humankind. Enjoy.

[ (Excerpt of a previous work)

The recorded history of lgbt is as old as recorded human history and expands to every reach of our planet. There isn't a society on earth with a recorded history, that doesn't refer to some aspect of an lgbt community. LGBT seems to have existed since humans have existed, and in every corner of the world.

UCLA / Burkle Center produced a world map of just a portion of this history, which can be found at:

https://www.unfe.org/sexual-orientation-gender-identity-nothing-new/

Societies with a recorded lgbt history include: Native American Great Plains Tribes, Mayans, the Igbo people of Nigeria, Angola, the Dem Rep of Congo, South Africa, Kenya, Portugal, Italy, Greece, Albania, Egypt, Iran, Saudia Arabia, India, Nepal, Russia, Korea, China, Indonesia.

Plato mentioned a 3rd gender in his memoirs. In ancient Greece, many in the ruling Senate were openly lgbt. An ancient Greek marble sculpture shows a well-endowed female reclining on a lounge with obvious male genitalia. Another portrays three nude transgender females standing together.

Hermaphroditus was portrayed in Greco-Roman art as a female figure with male genitals, and Aphroditus was said to have been a male Aphrodite originating from Amathus on the island of Cyprus and celebrated in Athens in a transvestite rite.

The prophet Muhammad referred to LGBT when he wrote his governing ordinances on inheritance for his society. The writings show he accepted gender nonconformity.

To quote a national leader, "Gay people are born and belong to every society in the world. They are all ages, all races, all faiths. They are doctors and teachers, farmers and bankers, soldiers and athletes. And whether we know it or whether we acknowledge it, they are our family, our friends, and our neighbors. Being gay is not a western invention. It is a human reality."

## The Religious / Biblical argument regarding LGBT Normality

### The *assumed* origin of the LGBT non-acceptance paradigm:   God. The Bible.

Easy as that. It doesn't matter what argument is made. No argument against God wins.

What if I can prove on many levels, God has NO problem with LGBT, and even calls them blessed and His blessed – in the Bible?

(Parts of this discussion will mention previously discussed subjects, but it must be included in this segment to offer the complete LGBT argument.)

### Proof God has no problem with LGBT

God's commandments have been discussed, and no matter what list you wish to adopt as authentic, or how many commandments you believe God gave, all the lists have one thing in common:

There is no commandment against LGBT. There are commandments about oxen …but none against LGBT.

Please remember, if God had wanted an eleventh …or …fifty-third commandment, She would have written one. God has the ability, and the rock to write on. There was and is nothing to stop God. Yet there is no commandment against LGBT. …None

I believe I've debunked the idea the original Bible authors transcended time and/or were divinely inspired. If they transcended time, they would have known slavery, stoning someone to death without trial, and female oppression and subjugation, are not acceptable.

>Deut 15: 12-15  Eph 6: 9  Col 4: 1  Deut 22: 22  Mark 10:1-12  Mark 12: 18-27  Exod 31:14-15  Deut 22: 13-21  Eccl 7: 2  Eccl 25: 18, 19, 33

Existential psychology states it is impossible to remove the society from the human. Neuroenterology and Epistemology have proven we think using our societal language, which is the primary representation of that culture, including time and location limitations.

The Positive and Negative Argument for LGBT Acceptance *within the Bible*

### The Positive Passages

Is God quoted in the Bible as saying anything good or positive about LGBT? Yes. Jesus said some are born gay. And the most impressive passage comes with its own written-in proof of authenticity and verification.

1. Matthew 19: 11-12 - ¹¹ But He (Christ) said to them, "Not everyone can receive this saying, but only those to whom it is given. ¹² For there are eunuchs who have been so from birth, and there are eunuchs who have been made eunuchs by men, and there are eunuchs who have made themselves eunuchs for the sake of the kingdom of heaven. Let the one who is able to receive this receive it."

Eunuch is a misinterpretation for: 'men not comfortable sleeping with women'.

– Males aren't born castrated. People are born gay.

– Castration does not serve heaven. Being gay can serve heaven.

The time-traveled (mis)interpretation of the word 'Eunuch' allowed the passage to remain untouched, but the passage is untouched for a spiritual reason: *Who is able to see the message.*

¹²"Let the one who is able to receive this receive it":

I understood the message immediately. Can you, or does God blur your attempt, so you may be tested by your heart alone?

The accepted, inaccurate current interpretation will allow the myopic to make their argument, the passage has nothing to do with LGBT. And their inability to understand has left the passage unaltered accordingly. The preceding and succeeding sentences prove it.

This passage is too amazing, in its message, its self-included verification, and its spiritual ramifications: The preceding and succeeding sentences are beyond this world. They validate the content AND explain our current failure to accept.

You cannot be taught the message. It's a test and measures your immortal maturity. You see it or you don't, but it absolutely without question, verifies God has no problem with LGBT. Their status serves heaven. It's as if the spiritual universe is using that community as a gauge to measure human maturity.

Other pro-LGBT Bible passages
1. Matthew 8: 5-13 - Jesus Affirmed a Gay Couple
    The 'servent' was the soldier's male lover
2. Ruth 1: 14 - Ruth loved Naomi
3. Acts 8: 26 – 40 - The early church welcomed gay men
    'Eunuch' is again a misinterpretation for 'gay man'.
4. 1 Sam 19-23 & II Sam 1 & 9 - David loved Jonathan more than women
    The interpretation is complex, but they aren't just friends
5. Luke 17: 34-37 - Christ blessing gay relations
    [34]I tell you, in that night there shall be two men in one bed; the one shall be taken and the other shall be left.

³⁵There will be two women grinding. One will be taken and the other left.

(The one taken – is taken to HEAVEN) – But why? Aren't they GAY? Aren't the GAY cursed? Aren't the GAY condemned to hell? Isn't it an **abomination**?)   ]

How is it, three pro-lgbt GOSPEL verses (two-directly attributed to Christ) are summarily dismissed, but three anonymously written old testament verses against LGBT (one in the middle of an all-but-ignored childlike diatribe) are held to like commandments?

When someone tells you, being LGBT is against God / God is against LGBT, ask them: What does **Christ** say about LGBT in the Bible? (I've proven: Every other associated bible passage is a *human* thought – some are from *anonymous humans*.)

Since the human you ask, won't know...

ANSWER: Matthew 19: 11-12 / Matthew 8: 5-13 / Luke 17: 34-37 - Christ not only has no problem with LGBT, but says God considers LGBT as normal as any other group of people. If you study and read into Christ's message, you will learn: God is using LGBT for His purpose.

How funny! I just realized Christ was LGBTQIA.

One of the apostles was purportedly gay – Christ's brother James.

[ **The Negative Passages**

The 6 Bible bullets that supposedly kill all LGBT and the bomb that wipes out all those shooting bullets:

**1 Cor 6:9   1 Tim 1:10   Lev 18:22*   Lev 20:13***

**Rom 1:26   Gen 19**

**1 Cor 6:9:** (This is previously discussed in 'Re-Writings and Re-Interpretations', and copied here. Please refer to that discussion for further detail)

[9] Or do you not know that wrongdoers will not inherit the kingdom of God? Do not be deceived: Neither the sexually immoral nor idolaters nor adulterers nor men who have sex with men[a]

[ ***Footnotes:**

a. 1 Corinthians 6:9: The words *men who have sex with men* translate two Greek words that refer to the passive and active participants in homosexual acts.   ]

* This footnote is in the notes on the Bible website and **not my footnote**.

- Operative Greek words in the original Greek document: "Malakoi" and "Arsenkoitai":

   * *THESE* are the two Greek words the footnote references.

— Malakoi's literal translation means 'weak willed' / 'gutless' / 'spineless' …was somehow **mistranslated** to: effeminate …as in sexually / genderly effeminate / gay / lgbt

— Arsenkoitai : Modern humans cannot find a literal translation for this highly uncommon and rare Greek word, but to declare its meaning: 'homosexuality' is once again more an adage against the interpreter than the Bible meaning. There were, at the time of original authorship, many words which meant 'homosexual' in the Greek language and if that's what the author wanted to convey, it is believed he would have used one of those many common words. He did not.

**1 Tim:** Authorship is in question. The prophesies in 1 Tim have been proven questionable. Linguistics reveal inaccuracies involving the time claimed written and the words and phrases used accordingly. This nullifies the document's authenticity.

**Leviticus** reads as if written by a person with the maturity of a five year old child. "Don't wear multi-fabric underwear"? Don't even trim your beard? Don't eat half the food God placed here for our enjoyment, or you're impure and condemned to eternal damnation? This is where you find the Leviticus edict against homosexuality. If this document was written today, we would laugh at the author before dismissing him and it.

* The Apostle Paul said, "Christ has set us free from the yoke (Leviticus) of slavery through Christ, you are no longer obligated to religious law." - Galatians 5:1.

**Romans:** One verse about homosexuality and eight condemning those criticizing their government. The document equally condemns deceit, pride, debate and disobedience. Please stop a moment and reflect on exactly what Paul is calling sinful. Are any of these things actually sins? Are any of these actions anything but normal human activity?

The document equates the sin of homosexuality to that of pride, debate, and disobedience. Let's consider the exact level of human action, these 'crimes' are, and question Paul's motive, and non-modern intellectual capacity before considering any of these concepts, sins.

But if you want to measure the mindset of the humans from that time and place, please note: It is a 'flogging offense' for a woman to hang washed laundry outside without male supervision, in that part of the world, in *current modern times*. And why is it Paul and his peers have no problem with slavery, or stoning a non-virgin woman to death, but have a problem with 'debate'?

**Genesis:** There are many inaccuracies in Genesis. Six day creation? The universe is a 14 billion year ongoing creation. The sun and earth are 4 billion years old. The 2nd creation story on page 2 of Genesis contradicts the 1st creation story. It is verified and enclosed: the use of Adam and Eve is a plagiarism from Zoroastrianism. The story of Noah is a plagiarism of the Epic of Gilgamesh, King of Uruk. Similar flood stories are found in multiple ancient societies throughout the world. These inaccuracies nullify any claim of 'divinely inspired', and thus nullify any significance, claim of time transcendence, or validity.

**And the nuclear bomb wiping out all remaining religious argument against LGBT.     Galatians 3:10**

(This is previously discussed)

https://biblethumpingliberal.com/2011/05/19/you-can%E2%80%99t-quote-leviticus-to-prove-god-hates-homosexuality/

(Referencing the website)

[     …There is, however, a big problem with quoting any Testament Law. The problem is, Christians are no longer under the Law. Christians do not live their Christian life by following the Testament Law. The Apostle Paul makes this abundantly clear. It is not something fabricated to win an argument, or made up in the twentieth century, or manufactured to get around something somebody doesn't like. It is clearly stated in the Greek scriptures.

The Apostle Paul wrote in Galatians:

[10] All who rely on observing the law are **under a curse**, for it is written: "Cursed is everyone who does not continue to do *everything* written in the Book of the Law." (Galatians 3:10)

If we rely on following the Law or insist on imposing it on others, we are under a *curse*. The passage above, Galatians 3:10, contains a quote from the Law itself, Deuteronomy 27:26. ]

Straight from the Apostle Paul, in the original Greek: The Law no longer applies. Christ eradicated the law as the new covenant.

The practical application of Gal 3: 10:

If someone condemns homosexuality and is clean-shaven, has a tattoo, eats pork or shellfish, or wears multi-fabric clothes – *they* are cursed by *their* edict. If someone holds to the literal translation of the Bible, they have cursed themselves. Per Gal 3:10 - you don't get to pick and choose which law you like and wish to adhere to and which law you don't. …So I advise we drop them all. Our eternal health demands it.

Leviticus 19 "The LORD said to Moses": [19] Do not wear multi-fabric cloth.

Half cotton, half polyester underwear offends God?

...Sounds just like I'd expect an eons old perfect universe creator to sound.

And if anyone is offended by the statement, please adhere to the law and not wear multi blend fabrics.

...Homosexuality: Both of them have committed an abomination." Lev 20:13

No they haven't. Homosexuality is as natural as heterosexuality. Two people loving each other is godlike. God is love. Two people making love under those terms, is natural, or it wouldn't work or be pleasurable...and it works and is pleasurable, or people wouldn't do it.

These paradigms need re-evaluation. Existing beliefs are failing our God and Her children...our brothers and sisters.

Better news: Old religious laws never were anything more than culturally based. Ancient middle-eastern societal leaders made the laws 'religious' for better tribal adherence. God isn't that petty or trite, and never has been. They are and always were human laws, not spiritual laws. Their religious connotation helped adherence. The Hebrews made their entire society religious, for law adherence and cultural purposes.

Buddhism is a religion for similar reasons. Gautama's teachings were being lost and an Indian nobleman knew the religious connotation would help his society keep the wisdom.

"Do not eat pork or shellfish" became Hebrew religious law because many were dying from eating tainted pork and shellfish. They had no refrigeration and lived in a desert.

But once and for all, Paul (not me) wipes archaic religious laws from existence, by word, or action of Christ, depending on your level of belief, which also has no bearing on your salvation. You're God's. It was a done deal from day one. …Just like your children are yours …from the instant they exist.

[ (Previous work continued)

It could be argued I'm just keeping the Bible parts I like and am comfortable with and throwing away the parts I'm not happy with. Why yes. And there is a reason. Some of the parts about completely pure perfect love of a completely pure perfect God make complete sense after I evaluated them, and some of the parts sound like a bad infomercial telling us about our incurable disease and offers the one and only solution. And God alone can't cure you. Only religion offers the cure. God doesn't have the ability alone, to help you honor the purported 'Sabbath' commandment, even though Christ spoke clearly about how to pray, in *The Sermon on the Mount*.

'I'm still not allowed to pick and choose what parts of the Bible I want to honor and what parts I don't.'

Why not? The religious have been doing this for quite some time. What is interesting about their choices is, the religious seem to ignore the Bible edicts they must adhere to, and hold against others, that which others must adhere to. The religious eat pork and shellfish. Religious males shave. Religious wear multi-fabric blend clothing. Many have tattoos. They hate. They judge. They used to wear veils but don't anymore. There used to be a law against work on the Sabbath which they now ignore with gusto. They are doing and have been doing exactly what I just did.

But I'm not saying they shouldn't ignore things they've already identified as antiquated and are currently ignoring. I'm actually saying there are more things to identify and ignore: Hate. Ignore the hate parts. Ignore anything that denies a human's right to exist. Condemning others…ignoring that one sounds like a great and healthy idea too, don't you think?

Please understand this discussion isn't an argument against religion. Religion's inability to project the unconditional perfect love and forgiveness that is God, is not my or this discussion's problem. That is religion's problem.

This is a discussion between 'love' and 'hate'; an argument about children too immature to understand they don't have the right or awareness to evaluate the existence of anything, let alone others. To judge another reflects only on the judge's immaturity. Christians do not fare well in Muslim eyes, just as Muslims don't fare well in Christian eyes. But the fault lies only in the judgement. Our entire planet is suffering from its growing hatred, and hatred's foundation is borne in judgement.

> Love is the absence of judgment. – Dalai Lama XIV
> So is forgiveness. –

The following links lead to much more profound and wordy discrediting discussions (some of which I offer partial credit for my knowledge and knowledge confirmation):
1. http://wouldjesusdiscriminate.org/biblical_evidence.html
2. https://biblethumpingliberal.com/gays-lesbians-in-luke/
3. http://www.wouldjesusdiscriminate.org/biblical_evidence/history_lessons.html
4. http://www.huffingtonpost.com/adam-nicholas-phillips/the-bible-does-not-condemn-homosexuality_b_7807342.html
5. http://wouldjesusdiscriminate.org/biblical_evidence/no_fems_no_fairies.html
6. http://www.religioustolerance.org/ashford01.htm
7. http://www.huffingtonpost.com/john-shore/the-best-case-for-the-bible-not-condemning-homosexuality_b_1396345.html

8.      https://www.google.com/search?q=Argument+refuting+anti+lgbt+bible+claims&ie=utf-8&oe=utf-8      ]

Moses seems to have had a problem with LGBT, if he's the Torah author, and to think his problem is God's, is unfounded. God made homosexuality and He makes _**no**_ mistakes. He's perfect, remember? Perfect Beings don't make mistakes, and the LGBT community has been on the face of the Earth since humans have, in every corner of the world…documented…in spite of an eons-long attempt to eradicate these brothers and sisters. LGBT doesn't exist in spite of God. *Nothing* exists in spite of God. It exists in spite of religion, and *because* of God. It is your great test, religious, and you're not faring well with regard to your God's wishes. Please reference John 13: 34-35.

Dear LGBT brothers, sisters, and children: You are normal. Your sexual preference is normal. People like you have existed since people have existed, and in every corner of the world. And anyone telling you differently has either not studied your culture and history, has adopted age-old unfounded human paradigms without forethought, or has selfish proclivities and agendas.

You can, 1 – ignore them. 2 – use God's words to kill their argument. 3 – beat them with their own religious book as you ask them what their definitions of love and the golden rule are.

If you choose option three, please understand it may be the closest they've ever come to touching their religious book, so they may continue trying to avoid it as if its touch was poisonous.

The mass genocide against the LGBT sub-culture needs to come to an end. The exclusion of this sub-culture from mainstream society needs to come to an end. And unless you get caught doing something you'd rather not get caught doing, their sexual preference has no effect on you whatsoever.

How easy is it to not be affected by the LGBT lifestyle?

If you personally don't want to have sexual relations with someone of the same gender, by all means, don't. Say, *No thank you*, and then leave that other person to her or his life…and stay out of their bedroom. Please don't judge. Their Maker has the full ability, authority, and responsibility, and He doesn't need your help or opinion on the validity of His children.

Please stop thinking, God is so imperfect, She would create something He hated. The idea does not align with the acknowledgement of a *perfect* God.

And if your heart beats faster when thinking about how wrong homosexuality is, or how disgusting it would be if a same-gender person offered you the opportunity to be intimate, don't take a psychology course on sexuality, or you're going to learn things you're going to inwardly deny for the rest of your life.

In a recent study, 50% admit to some form of LGBT experimentation. Psychology knows: Vociferous unsolicited vocalization against, usually means a secret disposition toward. Indifference is the actual reaction of those unaffected and disinterested.

And a place that equally allows one to marry their same gender partner, and be fired for it the next day, is ruled by children lost in their own childishness. Equality isn't hard to comprehend, but if you're having difficulty comprehending, you've shared more about you than you should have.

Practical perspective:

A four year old child wanted a toy, and when her mother told her they didn't have the money, she replied, "Then just go to the money machine and get some."

The four year old knows where money comes from, right?

Humans are cosmically this child. Can we please begin realizing God knows just a little more than we do, about *everything*? Why do we see what God has created and decide it isn't exactly what He intended?

Youth: The elderly are half as smart because they've lived twice as long. –

Humans: We know how God has failed, because God is timelessly older, wiser, and smarter. –

Our cosmic mental age is showing.

And if you don't want to use a 'clinic' …don't. But please don't stop another from using it. Their life is no one else's business. Their life is between them and their Maker. This isn't a new rule. This has been called **_'The Golden Rule'_** since the beginning of time. If your guardians never taught you the golden rule, here it is:

**_Do unto others as you would have them do unto you._**

Did you know Christ said it?

[12]"So whatever you wish that others would do to you, do also to them." – Matthew 7:12

[8]the royal law found in Scripture, "Love your neighbor as yourself" – James 2: 8

Do you want to be left alone, to go about your life without others interfering with your actions and beliefs? … Picture others forcing you to adopt their beliefs. How uncomfortable is the feeling? Would you strike out against it? Would you insist to be left alone, but treated as equal?

Some have already insisted on 'religious tolerance' laws which allow them to discriminate based on their religious beliefs. Many of these people believe in things like conversion therapy for LGBT. …Christ's teachings or the precepts of men? (Mark 7: 6-8)

Live and let live?

We should live by our rules and answer to our Maker, and allow others to live by their rules and answer to their Maker. And as much as our preachers insist it's our duty to inform heathens of their eminent destination, for whatever religious laws they're not honoring – it is not. All we will have done by sharing that bit of information is: put a curse on our own head. We will, by our words, have subjected ourselves to religious Law. I've seen heathens' destination and there's a good chance some of us are mistaken about their fate. And if there's no refuting proof, we should lower our adamant volume.

And when a clean-shaven preacher stands in front of you wearing a cotton polyester shirt with sleeves short enough to see his beautiful 'I love Jesus' tattoo, wearing a silk tie, and cotton polyester pants, having just come from a bacon and egg breakfast served in the church basement, with plans to attend the church barbeque later that evening, and tells you how homosexuality is an abomination, you can whisper in his ear after his performance, that he just cursed himself, and ought to read his own reference book.

[12] There is only one lawgiver and judge, He who is able to save and to destroy. But who are you to judge your neighbor? – James 4: 12

## The intellectual argument for LGBT Normality

(a continuation of the previous work)

[ **MEDICAL**

The medical / biological aspects of lgbt are enlightening. We've come a long way, with regard to studying and measuring human functionality. We used to take still pictures of the physical brain. We now make movies of the brain as it functions. We used to be able to identify hormones. We now watch them go about their assignment in the human body. Not long ago, we discovered the cell and its inner components. We now look into cell nuclei and then into its housed chromosomes and identify each marker on each level of each strand.

In that time, psychology moved from a newly formed pseudo-science with its foundation mired in social directive, to a far more objective and scientific social science, and has recently made great strides in disassociating itself from unmeasured societal hearsay and influence.

**MEDICAL / PSYCHOLOGICAL FINDINGS**

Modern medicine has recorded gender ambiguity at birth for as long as medical science has been inclined. 1 child in every 2500 is born physically gender unspecific, gender ambiguous and or multi-gendered. Our medical community immediately operates on these babies to 'remedy' their 'problem'. It is never discussed past the immediate family. Almost always, the child never knows its own birth situation. The idea a gender is assigned at birth is a medical ethics shortcoming for another discussion.

We as a society just recently realized that if this is the physical norm for as far back as has been recorded, why wouldn't the gender ambiguity also include the four other aspects of human existence? And the desire for the answer has led to some amazing findings such as biological psychology's identification of at least 18 distinct and different gender variations.

Advancements in medical technology have now given us the ability to measure gender nonconformity in all aspects of human existence and so far, it has identified the incidence of gender variation at roughly 1 in every 100 humans. This revelation has led to what some believe is a more fluid gender continuum than previously thought and completely wipes out the 2000 year old middle eastern belief that the proposed Maker made only man and woman.

**Klinefelter Syndrome**

**Turner Syndrome** - XO Chromosome pairing

**Complete Androgen Insensitivity Syndrome** (CAIS)

**Super Males** - XYY

Not even the ancient Greeks, Chinese or Native Americans believed we were just man and woman. Unquestioned beliefs proposed by radicals under friendly threat have driven us intellectually backward beyond primitive cultures and there are those who still get offended by the declaration.

My awareness allows me to believe the proposed Maker hasn't ever done anything dichotomously. Not only is every color of the spectrum on display everywhere we look, but there are colors so vast, and out of our sight spectrum, we're not sure where or if they end. It is measured that we see roughly 400 points of a spectrum that is almost infinity wide. We have at one invisible end, the infrared and beyond and the other invisible end, the ultraviolet and beyond. And we know specifically, certain other animals can see different spectrums than humans. The same variance applies to sound, smell, taste, and touch.

God's creative imagination is not limited nor is it self-restricted. Our ability to comprehend God's creative imagination is limited and we are working hard to keep it self-restricted. We are all different in every way possible. Some find that fact disappointing. I think it's fascinating.

We also fall inside a law we have hoped not to: the law of physical creation. We would like to believe we are above that universe encompassing law. We would hope we are unique and not bound by the laws that bind lower life forms. We would like to believe we're closer to the top of sentient existence than the bottom, for reasons beyond existential proof. ... Ego, inflated self-worth …points for another discussion. If it can exist, it most likely does. If there are limitations to physical existence, we are well ensconced within those boundaries. Is any of it an accident? Topic for an interesting future discussion, but my argument and perspective is, The Definition of Perfect.

So unlike antiquated tribes who thought the Earth was alone in the cosmos, and angels raised the sun each morning, I now get to marvel at Hubble telescope pictures of galaxies too numerous to count, now excitedly, with planets also too numerous to count. And am able to contemplate our inner being's continuum of countless types measuring the range of spectrum the Maker has displayed everywhere else. Are the physical parameters greater than we currently understand? Without a doubt. Can we comprehend even their possibility of existence? We're children in the cosmic scheme who aren't yet mature enough to stop abusing the planet we're not advanced enough to leave en masse. Considering we're also blowing each other up for no apparent reason, I'd say that sets our cosmic age somewhere less than we'd initially guess.

### THE NATURE ASPECTS

#### THE PSYCHOLOGICAL *5 PART BEING* CONCEPT
Psychology has broken down human existence into 5 inner aspects. They are physical, mental/intellectual, emotional, spiritual,

and social. Here is a quick perspective of the five, with regard to lgbt.

**Physical**

2000 years ago, certain specific cultures believed there were just men and women. I have already proven to you that many other cultures believed otherwise, but I make that statement and that specific past time identifier for a reason. We as a culture seem to have given a certain 2000 year old middle eastern culture carte blanche with our inherent belief system, including our societal beliefs. But unlike those ancient beliefs, modern doctors, psychiatrists, biological psychologists, psychology, medicine, and biology all offer new and different perspectives on lgbt and all agree on one point. LGBT is just another normal healthy human variation.

If however, you are one of the people these modern facts with verification confuse because of certain foundational beliefs, let me offer… Is there anyone who has not witnessed an effeminate male and or a masculine female in their lives? That quickly makes 2 genders 4. Now with that new awareness, is there anyone who can't imagine, identify, or recognize levels of masculinity and femininity in both males and females? It's not easy until the differences are so obvious they cannot be denied, but science has proven the male female difference is not stepped or scaled, but a continuum, from different opposing aspects. Did you know there are both male and female hormones in every male and female and we couldn't survive without the 'opposite sex' hormones operating within us?

With a more thorough examination, it seems the Great Maker made us more homogeneous than we'd like to think. Humans aren't just male and female. That is an old tribal belief, and it may be time we use the findings of our comprehensive modern educational system to advance past certain antiquated tribal beliefs.

**Mental/Intellectual**

Psychology links its sub-domains together because it believes any one domain affects the others. The unique mental aspect of certain children who fit into the lgbt community is something any good psychologist will tell you is beyond the comprehension of people outside this community. It took a prominent and gay psychologist to prove beyond a doubt that being lgbt isn't a mental disorder, as was initially believed and included in the psychology bible, the Diagnostic and Statistics Manual or DSM, and this also cries out to the inherent cultural influence and inaccuracy of certain foundational beliefs.

The thought synopsis is, if you haven't lived it and experienced it yourself, you don't know what it feels like.

We can empathize, we can do our best to comprehend, we can accept, but we cannot know. So if we do not know, why do we all have opinions with a significant percentage of us refusing to accept this community wholeheartedly?

**Emotional**

The self-revelation that one fits into this community is the spectrum of emotions, though on the negative side, the level of denial is unprecedented for any other sub culture. People hide behind heterosexual relationships, sneak around in risky places, or deny themselves to their dying day.

This is what we offer them as a culture, and my concern is the additional emotional discomfort our society has added to these individuals. It is fact that there have been societies who wholeheartedly accepted their lgbt community and even gave its normalcy little thought due to the complete acceptance level, and there have been societies like ours where acceptance is considered a sin. Conversely, the stigma felt emotionally by these individuals is nothing less than a sin and that sin is on our entire society. "If God is love, then isn't it better to love completely wrong than it is to hate completely right?" Jake to his mother, Chapter 13, The Definition of Normal.

**Spiritual** (non-religious)

If you believe in God, I'm assuming you believe as I do; God is perfect. God made no mistakes nor did God make things just so God could hate and destroy them. God is the Creator. God gets no joy from destruction. Nothing can challenge God, so there would be no pleasure in the destruction.

God is love. You are loved. You are loved beyond your understanding. God is perfect, so God's capacity to love is incomprehensibly perfect from an imperfect being's perspective. God's capacity to love is beyond your capacity to comprehend.

Under those terms, you are exactly what God chose to make and if you are lgbt, which God has chosen to sprinkle from one end of the earth to the other since the beginning of man, then you are exactly what God intended to make…and at that point, if you are non lgbt and don't agree, then it isn't God who needs further comprehension. If you don't agree, it is not lgbt who need further evaluation. If you don't agree, and you haven't bothered to self-evaluate your beliefs, examining them for validity and legitimacy, but only blindly accept what you've been fed without discerning thought, then you are forgiven and loved just the same.

We only hope in time, you have a change of heart. But understand GOD is perfect and you are here to learn lessons. Your growth as a cosmic being is based on learning these lessons. There is no punishment associated with the failure to do so. Only the edict, you do not advance as a spiritual being until the lesson or lessons are learned.

And if you don't believe in God, then someone else's lifestyle, which doesn't hurt or harm you in any way, should not be a single thought, good or bad, in your entire repertoire of thought.

**Social**

There are two aspects to the social.

**1.** How our being is fed by social interaction. We have proof that a weakening or separation of social connection leads to inner health issues and can be an indicator of a future suicide attempt. The inner health the social aspect brings has been noted psychologically. There is an inner force which is fed by social connection. We are social beings.

**2.** It is an outside force that is well recorded. Our word society is a derivative. It has its own field of study. It is obvious.

Denying someone the ability and/or right to enjoy full social standing and participation in our society is cruel and unfair. To make someone feel socially inferior because of who they are, whether by color, creed, nationality, religion, gender, or sexual preference is immature at best… harmful at worst. None of us are perfect. None of us are everything we want to be. But not having the nerve to speak when someone else declares another inherently inferior is disheartening to anyone who believes all people are created by a perfect maker and in that Being's eyes – equal.

Our society has distressingly incongruent messages regarding equality. One of my favorite is the 3$^{rd}$ line of the Declaration of Independence: "We hold these truths to be self-evident, that all men are created equal."

We teach the concept of equality to our 4th graders as if it's law. As a 4th grader, I bought it. Five decades later, there is still no implementation.

### The Nurture Aspect of the Nature Nurture Argument

We like to believe we are a nurturing society. In fact, some parts of our society who insist they're the most nurturing are not only failing this aspect of their existence, but their thoughts and actions are causing our children to panic with the false realization they're 'condemned to eternal hell'.

When this group is questioned regarding their beliefs, their response is, "It's just our opinion." Sadly, just their opinion that others are doomed to eternal hell, comes with a death toll and body count. Our lgbt children are committing suicide at a rate four times greater than average. 'Just their opinion' it seems …is not 'just their opinion'. If it was, they would keep it 'just to themselves', but no, it's shared as loudly as possible. Why? They would like 'just their opinion' to be everyone's opinion, not unlike certain radical other religions who would like all humans to be restricted to another set of confusing archaic religious laws created during a less than advanced time, in a less than advanced place, by a less than advanced culture.

I'm not asking you to change years of thought process in a moment, a day, or a week, but I am asking you to understand some of the things we believe are not healthy for us or others and maybe it's time we adjust our thinking.

Any two humans holding hands or kissing is not offensive. Any two humans making disparaging motions or remarks about two humans holding hands or kissing is offensive. Any two humans showing affection is not offensive. Any two humans stopping two humans from showing affection is offensive. It's not what God taught. ]

Many theologians believe the Bible passages referring to homosexuality, don't condemn consensual homosexual activities.

I apologize, but I'm still curious why *anyone* thinks they have the authority to judge another. Refusal to judge another should be a basic social paradigm, but for those who don't find it inherently basic, ancient wisdom shares the instructions.

# Chapter Thirteen
## Legacy of Religion

There was a time when the original Christian religious organization forbade owning a bible. Could a reason be, they were aware of the discrepancies within the book and were concerned the discrepancies would be discovered by their followers? The punishment for this disobedience was death, and religion murdered thousands. The organization's earthly agenda became so blatant and so intolerant, different sects of the Christian religion were founded.

The mindset behind religion's ongoing physical, mental, and spiritual oppression is hard to vindicate. No organization has imprisoned and killed more Christians than the largest, oldest Christian organization. No organizations have killed more Muslims, than the two largest Muslim organizations, and there are countless deaths attributed to both sides in their ongoing atrocities against each other, though both acknowledge their brotherhood. These two religions have committed murder on a genocidal level.

Love/Forgive? You would expect the grand-scale harm God's children have endured, to be the work of organizations opposing God.

Neither religion has ever shown a communion with God. God is love. Neither religion is love. God is forgiveness. Neither religion is forgiveness (without ritual and/or donation).

Both exclude groups of God's children, based on their man-made laws. Both embrace rituals that would make the Sadducees proud. Both religions exclude those of other religions, even when those other religions worship the same God.

I've been waiting for these organizations to make one simple statement showing they know God and from inception to today, have never heard or read a single-deity religion unsolicitedly state:

'God and this religion accept all God's children as God has made them. Unconditionally. Not only are all welcome to be part of our family, but we would rejoice by your joining and would cherish our chance to love and accept each other in fellowship, without judgment, obligation, or intention to change. Unconditional acceptance … nothing more, nothing less.'

That's who God is. If that isn't the point-of-view of the organizations swearing to represent God …then they don't represent God. I've been given an instant's glimpse of who God is, and I've studied religion. I not only find it impossible to argue, religion knows God, but I've easily found countless examples for the opposite argument.

With regard to their ongoing genocides: God gave each religion a handful of commandments, and murder is the single most egregious offense.

I can't help but think religious organizations know every fact and understand every perspective they currently misinterpret. I can't see how they wouldn't. This information is easily found and studied. Their sole existence is supposedly based on interpreting who God is, and conveying that to the world. Thousands of years, billions of dollars and billions of people with the primary purpose to do what took me a few decades to discover. How could they not know the true meaning…the true purpose of God…His true nature and message?

Further discussion on Bible history, origins, and religion's human quotient can be found at:

http://www.religioustolerance.org/
http://www.religioustolerance.org/imm_bibl.htm

Other discussions on bible verse duplications, ghost writers, forgeries, the origins and perspectives of antiquated forgeries, and perspectives on the time/place origins of bible writings can be found with little effort, if desired.

## The Earth's Dilemma

I hear the pious religious claim, 'our human problems are because we're not as religious as we need to be. Non-religious, LGBT, and in general, people behaving unreligiously are ruining everything. Heathens are ruining everything. We need to get back to God!'

First, we need to establish, do these people mean the vindictive ogre god with all the adherence rules, or the love/forgive God I've been introduced to? If they mean the *perfect* love/forgive God …they can use this document to help their cause, but these (above) assumptions would first need adjusting.

I look forward to also hearing these religious mentioning their aversion to the hate, religion is spreading …the exclusion …the purposeful divide they're creating … the outrage religious display when other groups win inalienable rights they've enjoyed their entire lives.

Our human problem isn't church attendance or lack of prayer. It's hate. Hate opposes all God is. Even the most well-intentioned hate.

Humans are solely responsible for our world's dilemmas. We hold the cure, and our refusal to recognize our responsibility speaks volumes to who we are as a species. Our physical actions against our planet are now beginning to show. Our social actions against each other, compound our dilemma.

We're more in control of our fate than we care to acknowledge. Like children, we don't want to admit it's time to be accountable, and the potential result will be our own doing.

Loveless religious zealousness is more responsible for our dilemmas than the heathen and non-religious they blame. But it's human nature to blame others for what's wrong. God teaches to look inward first.

What did the Christ say about the plank in our own eye, before addressing the splinter in another's?

Treat each other as if we're all going to die in a short time, and maybe it won't happen. –

**Tolerance and Acceptance**

It is completely acceptable for people to believe in things which aren't accurate. It is acceptable for people to refuse to learn and grow as sentient beings. This becomes unacceptable when people force their beliefs on others.

How can we convince religion to adopt a more mature and spiritual understanding of God?

I offer the possibility, a new and more mature understanding of *Perfect* can lead this process. From that single foundation, maybe we can readjust our thinking accordingly.

I'm not suggesting we offer religious organizations, negative ramifications for their actions. I hope they see our intentional forgiveness and offer the human race, reciprocating kindness.

Humans are far more diverse than our current antiquated religions acknowledge. Can we reconsider trusting our *perfect* God, and begin accepting His creation diversification?

We forgive you, religious. Can you love humans enough to readjust your message?

**Coexist**

Please consider the idea we should live by our choice of rules while allowing others to live by their choice of rules. Our rules are not better or worse than their rules. Rules aren't meant to be compared. Don't compare. Don't judge.

– Coexist –

And if others' rules conflict with or differ from our rules, please allow those groups to coexist. And if others' rules differ, but don't hurt or oppress, please allow those groups to coexist.

We should abandon the rules which hurt or oppress others, before God shares lessons which would be beneficial to avoid. God is patient with transgressions, even using them to teach others, but there comes a time when spiritual authority decides, one groups' lessons are sufficient and concern is turned toward others requesting lessons through their actions.

If you think you've bypassed your lessons, through faith, or you're absolved from learning lessons, through faith, you're inviting lessons which would be best to avoid.

Our God is love/forgive, and this is what She teaches. We can voluntarily decide to coexist or we can invite lessons which will teach us coexistence. God wishes His children to love/forgive. Culturally, coexistence represents the first step in the spiritual edict.

We've been given signs of ancient advanced civilizations, here on earth. What do you think happened to those civilizations? Can you contemplate the idea that lessons are repeated until they're learned?

[5]Blessed are the meek, for they will inherit the earth.
[7]Blessed are the merciful, for they will be shown mercy.
[9]Blessed are the peacemakers, for they will be called children of God.
Matthew 5: 5,7,9

**Observations**

If the F bomb offends you or makes you gasp but not the N word, I humbly request you consider adjusting your paradigms. The F bomb isn't offensive. Words that offend are offensive. Words that hurt are offensive. We all know them. They demean someone's origin, ethnicity, gender, sexual preference, color, religion, physical being. The list is established. The F bomb doesn't make the list. It only offends the pretentious, and many inoffensive things offend the pretentious.

Are there places not to use it? Yes. The mature know the different places where it's polite not to use and necessary *to* use.

There are times it helps make a person's point, don't you think?

Some believe our physical being is made in the image of God, but we have a gender and a physical form. God has neither. Our spiritual being may look like God's, but we don't know that either. But why would this matter? Don't you think our desire for imitation should focus on the non-physical aspects of this perfect Being?

Learned Intelligence

Thoughts on the difference between the studied, and the unstudied, and how it relates to learning specific subjects:

To think people who've studied their chosen subject to great extent, and those who haven't studied the referenced subject, know the same depth and perspective about the given subject, is a great hindrance to our advancement.

Education and intelligence are not synonymous, but indicators favor the educated being more aware of what intelligence entails. Higher education teaches an awareness of knowledge in general. The educated have more awareness of and connection to recently discovered information, and are far more familiar with the new information verification process.

Media is now allowing non-experts to gain attention, assume notoriety, and feed false equivalency. Please measure the source of your information.

Sociology teaches, read information enters the analytical side of the brain while listening to information enters the emotional side. Objective information dissemination is not helped by a human medium.

The generation in charge has been given more knowledge and resources than any other generation, yet has done more harm to humanity than any other generation. Benevolent systems have been bastardized. Why?

Those who've tried to separate and divide are teaching what division and oppression create, and have put the opposite into motion. They served their purpose and their names are on their deeds. They'll be remembered, but not like they think.

Those who've done so in the name of God, have also tainted God's legacy and alienated His children.

When a child asks, why …and you answer: 'Because I said' / 'Because I'm older' / 'Because I'm the parent' / 'Because I'm bigger' – you're bullying.

Where do you think our children learn bullying? Please stop teaching them how to bully. Please stop being their first bully.

May I suggest a better approach? Answer questions with the reasoning supporting the statement prompting their question.

Your children can't hear your words. Your actions are deafening. –

Religious: Are you speaking against the hate being vocalized or are you quietly watching inequality from a distance? I know you think it isn't your place to worry about social injustice, when you have more important concerns. I'm not sure what specifically, but I see you sacrificing some of your most cherished beliefs, for those concerns. Please share what you're so afraid of losing, you would voluntarily ransom half of your beliefs, to secure. Maybe then, the rest of us will understand your fears better and be able to support you.

To the Parents of Imperfect Children

Please understand, using any set of human standards to abandon a child is a mistake. To use the Bible or God as an excuse to abandon your imperfect children – is a severe mistake. This includes the refusal to love.

Have you let your child know she or he is less than you can accept? ...Their lifestyle is offensive? So are you less than your child hoped. They hoped to be loved unconditionally, and their lifestyle may have meaning you can't comprehend.

God knows exactly what She has given you. (see: Perfect) It's your test. If you've chosen rules over love: Change immediately. Accept immediately. Love unconditionally, immediately. ...or hope your coming lessons don't astound you.

This needs re-emphasizing: God gave you a child to care for and be responsible for, like you were once a child, brought into this world without your consent, and hoped to be loved. Like you hope your heavenly Father loves and cares for you.

Deciding to have a child without pretense, then deciding she or he doesn't meet your acceptance standards, opposes all God is and has taught. You didn't decide to have the child …only if it's a boy, only if it's healthy, only if it's obedient, only if it's (fill in whatever word you'd like) …you decided to *have a baby*. You'll never be further from God in any action, than when you reject your child for not being – anything.

1) There was a father whose young son insisted on wearing a pink one-piece dance suit, and the caption on the picture: 'I realized that if I'm going to truly love my son I have to let him be true to himself. If that means he wants to be a ballerina in pink, my only concern is that he's the prettiest damn one anybody's ever seen.'

(Don't be concerned whether or not this is a real event. Measure the words.)

2) A wife and mother tells a story about her construction-worker husband: Their young son wanted his nails painted and after the mother obliged, they were going to a store, and the child felt embarrassed to go out with his nails painted, so the father painted his too. And the wife's response: 'He was never more masculine or more impressive than that moment'. (True story)

Fathers, be man enough to accept your child, for whatever she or he is. *What she or he is, has no bearing on your masculinity* ...unless your masculinity is so weak, it is already in jeopardy.

If someone questions your masculinity under these terms, please consider using that line to quell their condescension.

[8]Anyone who does not provide for their relatives, and especially their own household, has denied the faith and is worse than an unbeliever. – 1 Timothy 5:8

To Those Fighting Change

You grew up segregated. Your children don't. You grew up not living with anyone but those of your religion, ethnicity, race, sexual orientation, but your children don't. You grew up without seeing an unhealthy peer. They were cared for, away from the masses during your formative years, but not your children. Your children know them, grew up with them, and learned with them. Your children know these individuals are nothing more than unfortunate peers.

You learned fears regarding these differences, but your children didn't. So when you tell your children, they're not like people from different orientations, they know better, even though they tell me they don't necessarily share their more mature perspective with you. They know individuals representing the people you describe. Some are friends. Some are more than friends, though they don't tell you.

You've affected change in wonderful ways, but not like you think. Did you really think we could stop God's plan to move the world forward? There is only change, no matter how much we disagree with God's will.

Look backward. Do you see the points in time when humans struggled moving forward? Why would you wish similar struggles on the current generations?

I'd tell you your self-centered ways need to change, but they don't. They're about to die with your generation.

55% favor LGBT equality and marriage. Those under 25: 85%

55% believe in non-binary gender equality. Those under 25: 90%

60% favor bi-racial marriage. Those under 25: 90%

70% favor women's rights. Those under 25: 94%

70% believe in a more comprehensive definition of equality. Those under 25: 90%

Our children have full intentions of changing our world when their time comes. Their separation from antiquated beliefs has already begun. We can see it if we know where to look. It's a change some are trying to prevent and they're voicing their concern rather loudly regarding their inability.

But be happy for our children. They've already learned lessons some haven't learned their entire lives.

To the Wealthy

Greed is a peculiar conundrum, isn't it? You know it harms everyone. You know it destroys capitalism. You know greed is the argument for and precursor to socialism, yet you can't stop yourself from being ensnared in it. It's the most powerful human weakness.

If you think your riches are a reward, I'm sorry to inform you they're not. They're an assessment like everything else. And failing to learn this lesson is exactly like failing any other. The Lord explained to you in detail, your responsibilities regarding much given, and failure to adhere to God's wishes will earn you the lessons that accompany that failure.

If you think denying jobs or living wages and then giving people charity is fair compensation, please be careful. You're showing a need for lessons you might wish to avoid.

Are you a billionaire or millionaire denying people who work for you, a living wage? You have special mention in the Bible!

'But we operated within the rules.' –

— Whose rules?

Can you imagine what it's like having no opportunity to provide for yourself? Can't you understand the other side until you've experienced it? Do you think you have what you have for any other reason than to measure how you handle it?

Your resulting conundrum: Can you learn lessons softly today, so you don't receive harsher lessons tomorrow? Actions have a range of consequences, and we get to choose ours.

"A life of privilege requires actions to balance the harm caused, and the greater the privilege, the greater the responsibility. For if one does not leave behind a world better for having lived in it, all that remains are selfish ends, sometimes wrapped in family or nation." – David Buckel

Societal misconceptions regarding wealth:

An inaccurate puritan belief: Wealth is our way of knowing we please God and have His favor. (The Bible says the opposite)

This belief has led to other misconceptions:

– Wealth equals intelligence and/or righteous living.

– We can trust the wealthy to lead us.

– The wealthy will be benevolent leaders because they understand they've been given much.

Gautama's teaching: The middle road is the wisest, most pleasurable, beneficial path.

Nations are most prosperous when the middle class is most prevalent, and most successful. If you doubt this, look at the history of the world and nations. Notice when nations prosper, then decline.

Some leaders believe our rich are too poor and our poor are too rich. You'll identify them by their mandates for the rich and against the poor.

Our global economic dilemma

The wealthy siphon the circulating public resources into personal uncirculating coffers and this removal of resources strains the global economic network. Some wealthy profess it is the poor and social programs causing this shortage. It's easy to see why they'd want to divert us from the truth.

Solution: 1954 tax laws. The problem was already identified and a solution enacted. It was redacted as a result of the political marriage between the wealthy and powerful.

[2] Suppose a man comes into your meeting wearing a gold ring and fine clothes, and a poor man in filthy old clothes also comes in. [3] If you show special attention to the man wearing fine clothes and say, "Here's a good seat for you," but say to the poor man, "You stand there" or "Sit on the floor by my feet," [4] have you not discriminated among yourselves and become judges with evil thoughts? James 2: 2-4

⁵Listen, my dear brothers and sisters: Has not God chosen those who are poor in the eyes of the world to be rich in faith and to inherit the kingdom he promised those who love him? ⁶ But you have dishonored the poor. Is it not the rich who are exploiting you? James 2: 5-6

¹⁵ Suppose a brother or a sister is without clothes and daily food. ¹⁶ If one says to them, "Go in peace; keep warm and well fed," but does nothing about their physical needs, what good is it? ¹⁷ In the same way, faith by itself, if it is not accompanied by action, is dead. ¹⁸ But someone will say, "You have faith; I have deeds." Show me your faith without deeds, and I will show you my faith by my deeds. ¹⁹ You believe that there is one God. Good! Even the demons believe that—and shudder. James 2: 15-19

⁵ Now listen, you rich people, weep and wail because of the misery that is coming on you. ³You have hoarded wealth in the last days. ⁴ Look! The wages you failed to pay the workers who mowed your fields are crying out against you. The cries of the harvesters have reached the ears of the Lord Almighty. ⁵ You have lived on earth in luxury and self-indulgence. You have fattened yourselves in the day of slaughter. ⁶ You have condemned and murdered the innocent one, who was not opposing you. James 5: 1-6

[11] John answered, "Anyone who has two shirts should share with the one who has none, and anyone who has food should do the same." Luke 3:11

In a country well governed, poverty is something to be ashamed of. In a country badly governed, wealth is something to be ashamed of. – Confucius

Why aren't certain countries ashamed of both?

**Belittling Religion**

A powerful religious leader says we shouldn't belittle others' religion. But there's a death toll and body count from religious belittling certain other social groups. It's a primary factor for the suicide rate of LGBT children.

Dear religious leader: May I suggest you address your house first?

I'm sorry if it sounds like I'm belittling your religion. I'm not. I'm only sharing how religion divides, hates, murders, and puts burdens on lives. Actions God specifically spoke and acted against. If that sounds like belittling, please understand it's your religions' actions failing to withstand the scrutiny of God's edicts.

The fact I'm the one addressing it, has nothing to do with me. Religion is being measured against words directly attributed to those, religion has declared God's, and/or those religion has declared divinely inspired by God, and time-transcendent. If this document belittles your religion, using those words, maybe your religion belittles itself by failing to adhere to the teachings of its own God.

My secondary motivation for this document, is the hope these entities see their misguided direction, and change. If at any time, your religion or you don't like the truth, by all means, change.

Religion has not acknowledged or adjusted its immaturity for two thousand years, and I'm voicing curiosity. Why?

If it's because they can't see their activities, I want to help by illuminating their actions. Humans don't know to put a band-aid on a wound until the wound is identified.

If noting certain religious practices is belittling specific religions, and religion cannot handle the scrutiny, why aren't people acknowledging, that's religion's problem? If religion wasn't perpetuating childish antiquated practices, no one would be able to ask them why they're acting childishly. When organizations supposedly operating under a higher standard, stop their childish ways, those questioning them won't sound so …belittling.

Should anyone mind you adhering to your religious rituals? No. I once knelt until my knees hurt, and you're welcome to do the same. Your fate won't suffer for your actions. Perform any ritual you deem necessary to acquire what God has already guaranteed you. ...And know you're perfectly fine with your efforts, as long as they harm no one. But many religious aren't quite there yet. Many use their religious standing to belittle others.

May I humbly ask those with a tendency to pray to anyone but God: Please pray to God. When you're sick, you don't go to the doctor's mother or distant cousin. You go to the doctor. *The Sermon on the Mount* will help you understand what words to use and who to pray to, if you're unsure of either.

The Weak and the Strong

[14] Accept the one whose faith is weak, without quarreling over disputable matters. [2] One person's faith allows them to eat anything, but another, whose faith is weak, eats only vegetables. [3] The one who eats everything must not treat with contempt the one who does not, and the one who does not eat everything must not judge the one who does, for God has accepted them. James 14: 1-3

[5] One person considers one day more sacred than another; another considers every day alike. Each of them should be fully convinced in their own mind. [6] Whoever regards one day as special does so to the Lord. Whoever eats meat does so to the Lord, for they

give thanks to God; and whoever abstains does so to the Lord and gives thanks to God.  James 14: 5-6

**The Multiple Generation Curse**

You will not be punished for your anger, you will be punished by your anger. – Buddha

It's not your descendants who are cursed when your actions call for cursing. It's you. What is believed costs others, costs you. What you did for and to others, you did for and to you. You don't bless or curse another human being. You bless or curse you. Could our original religious authors understand this? No. They couldn't understand the foundation of the lesson. Hopefully, the foundation for the adjustment of this belief is explained better in this manuscript.

Is the duration of the ramifications four or ten generations? Figure out who told the author before you decide the length of the consequences of your actions, but realize your actions and beliefs have implications. They aren't punishments or curses. They're lessons. And you're the recipient of the lessons you earn.

Just lessons …some strong, some mild, changing with our changing perspectives and our ability to learn. None are at the expense of God's love for you. None threaten your existence.

## To Muslim Brothers and Sisters

Dear Muslim brothers and sisters: Allah is a beautiful name for our God, and He is love—perfect love. When the prophet asked you to be a soldier for Allah, he didn't mean go murder people who aren't your sect of religion. He meant for you to stand up for Allah. To represent Allah with strength and courage! Please don't think the prophet meant, you should fight and kill God's other children…your brothers and sisters. Please don't think hatred represents Allah.

Allah considers murder a horrendous crime. It is believed, murder is the only crime not included in our blanket absolution. You represent Allah …you're a soldier for Allah when you stand as a representative of His perfection. Please love/forgive as Allah loves/forgives.

There was a time when Muslims ruled East and West Europe and history shows it was one of the most mature times in Europe. Many Muslim-ruled areas accepted all religions. The Muslims called those of other religions—People of the Book, and understood, though a different religion, people of the Book meant they worshipped the same God. What name we give God, doesn't matter. God is God and we're all His children.

I apologize for current nations who don't have the same maturity as you once showed, and I'm sorry we're still learning how to be brothers and sisters, but please consider the true meaning of

*God's soldier* and champion our perfect God. Show how perfect He is. Continue fighting for peace, love and acceptance across all human differences.

**To the Next Generation**

First, know I love you. I loved you before I met you, and then you showed me your hearts after we met, and my love deepened beyond expectation.

I softly, secretly tested you. I gave you freedoms the authority did not – and you proved yourselves worthy. I talked to you about inclusion and you championed me. I discussed tolerance and acceptance with you and you cheered it and me. You're more mature, gracious, kind, tolerant, and loving than anyone credits you.

But don't become proud of your awareness. Please remain humble in it and understand humility allows the message to remain strong and pure.

Also understand your work has only started, and you have a long way to go before you get the opportunity to put your beliefs into action. You can continue to change your world, or you can accidentally fall into established habits. Please pay attention and continue on your current track. You'll find it will serve you and your world very well.

You're not wrong even though your beliefs don't always align with preceding generations. There's enough on this planet for everyone to have a satisfying share. There is no human not worthy. There's no human so different they aren't equal. You believe that now. Please continue believing it.

A gift to you:

Climbing the Mountain

You're at the complex at the base of the mountain you wish to climb. It's a beautiful business complex completely devoted to the products and services directly related to climbing the mountain it's attached to.

You enter the complex, and knock on the first door. It's one of the biggest and prettiest doors in the complex and it's front / center. It's the showroom and office of an excellent map seller. You enter and upon inspection, notice he has maps of every size and color of the paths you could take up the mountain. He has piles of them! He can put jewels on the map so it's the prettiest map you ever saw. He has blue ones with green trails, and green ones with blue paths. He has fluorescent ones, paper ones, plastic ones. He even has some that double as a placemat for eating. His suit is beautiful. His office is beautiful. There are pictures on the walls of famous people buying his maps. He also has pictures of the places he's travelled from selling so many maps, he's rich! He talks assuredly and elegantly about all those he knows who've used his maps to climb the mountain, and he's friendly and willing to discuss anything about his maps and how they'll help you. But he seems to omit one small detail. He never climbed the mountain.

After marveling a while, you decide to explore the rest of the complex. ...and...

You decide to knock on another door. The gentleman behind it invites you in. His office isn't nearly as large or pretty. His face is also a little worse for wear. His clothes look like he wore them up a mountain.

You think silently, *this is a little disappointing.* ...You look around. He has no maps for sale. Instead, he has dirty tools lying around which you don't even recognize. You ask him about a map, and he's a kind soul. He tells you that you can and even should buy a map. He tells you, "I own a few maps, but there's a spot about a quarter mile up that has this crooked rock on the right side of the path that isn't on any map, and if you don't know it's there, you can really sprain your ankle and then you won't be able to go much further. And a little further up, there's a hole that's kind of hidden and if you step in it, you'll fall down a nasty crevice and could end up in the hospital, let alone not finishing your climb. In fact, if you go buy a map and bring it back, I'll circle their general locations for you. I'd hate to see you get hurt trying to reach the top."

His statements suddenly give you the idea, this guy might just know more than you first thought...so you ask, "Do you know other things I should know about trying to climb this mountain?" And he says, "Sure. I've climbed it umpteen times. I've worn different shoes, for example, and I've found a pair that's much better than all the others I've tried. I also know a lady who makes the best clothes for the climb. They're lighter than all the other clothes I've used, but they're actually warmer. They're not as pretty as some of the other stuff, but when you're climbing a mountain, looks don't matter much. It's really comfortable too. This is the jacket and pants."

You start realizing this guy may help you complete your climb, so you ask, "Would you consider coming with me and being my guide for the climb?"

"Sure. It's what I do. Do you have all the tools you'll need?"

"...There are tools I'll need?"

After leaving this second office, you're now curious about the first door and the map guy, so you go back and talk to him again and when you ask him about the other guy you visited, he tells you, "Oh yeah...I know him. He's a little strange. You don't need him. Many have climbed the mountain without him, and he's way more expensive than my maps. You can buy one of my maps for pennies, and many have climbed the mountain using nothing more than one of my maps. Look at the piles of maps I have, and he uses an old wrinkled one he made himself. Did I show you the red one with the paths lined in white? It's beautiful! …Let me get it. I think it's in this pile…"

"Well…maybe I'll just take your least expensive one."

And the map seller turns and offers the slightest knowing condescension …for your own good, "You're not sure you need my map? Well, let me tell you something. My maps are invaluable. Look at how successful I am. Doesn't that tell you everything you need to know about my maps?"

3 types of information:
    1. Information you know
    2. Information you know you don't know
    3. Information you don't know you don't know
        a. Information you're unaware of
        b. Information you think is correct, but isn't
      Step 1: Moving information from # 3 to # 2
      Step 2: Moving information from # 2 to # 1


Process   Meta-process
   Asking questions
      Establish where you are on the path to your goal
      Establish how to discover how to get further down the path
   o  Learning to be the question asker – the art of asking questions

- Finding those further down the road you wish to travel
- Asking everyone if they know anyone you could speak with
- Breaking down whole processes into workable sub-processes
- More specific questions get more specific answers
- The last question (always): Are there any questions I didn't ask that the answer would also help me?
- Always get a *consensus* of opinion, to avoid inaccurate single-perspective answers

I offer 3 pieces of advice I've learned from my experiences.

1. Never ask anyone behind you, how to get further down the road you're on.

2. Learn the difference between someone who has done the task, and someone who has only read about it, no matter how much they've read or what wonderful titles they've accumulated from their reading.

3. Continually reassess the process you're using, to get where you want to eventually be. The door with the jewels behind it may offer less than you first recognized, when you didn't know enough to look past the glitter.

**To my (our) 'Imperfect Children'**

I know you're more mistreated than your peers. Your burden is great…sometimes overwhelming. I know how awful it is to be different. I've come to know affliction, and I recognize your pain.

But do you understand the lessons you've already learned? Do you understand how phenomenal your awareness already is? Would you know how normal, people like you are, if you weren't who you are?

Please don't throw that away. Please don't abandon humanity. Please don't abandon your like brothers and sisters who struggle alongside you or will immediately follow, only to struggle like you, after you. They and we need you. You can offer perspectives that allow the rest of us to grow. If you have strength, you can teach great and wondrous lessons of love, acceptance, and normality. You can be the change you desperately wish.

While you struggle, record your lessons of pain and confusion. Record your observations. They're invaluable! You can be another voice of reason. Is it hard? What worthwhile endeavor isn't?

Remember: You don't have to journey alone. But your sisters and brothers will, if you leave us. Please don't leave us.

Know, the experience is how God teaches. It's how we learn—truly learn. You know. Look inside your heart and mind. Measure how deeply you know things others can't fathom.

At seventeen, I was a depressed teenager who self-harmed and wondered just how painful it could be to end my life. Right now, I'm lying on the couch, and can hear my husband reading our four year old a bedtime story using silly voices. Life gets better. Please be here to see it. – Anon

**To All Brothers and Sisters**

Women = men
Black = white
Muslim = Christian
Non-religious = religious
Tall = short
Poor = rich
Minorities = majorities
All Races, Creeds, Religions are equal.
All genders are equal.
All sexual preferences are equal.
If you can put humans in different categories – the different categories are equal.

"We hold these truths to be self-evident; that all men are created equal." – Thomas Jefferson – repeated by: A. Lincoln (*Gettysburg Address*) – M. L. King (*I Have a Dream* speech)

Truth should not depend on the color of your skin, your gender, your religion, or your sexual preference. God declares all human differences, equal. Have you identified the humans / human organizations teaching the opposing message?

God's message is plain and simple. All humans are equal. Recognize it. Even consider declining support for those endorsing opposing views.

If every human's equality isn't your opinion, please re-evaluate your current paradigms. Let me help if you struggle with this: Today we're in one set of categories. Our next trip here, we will find ourselves in other categories. We have wonderful lessons to learn.

We are not in competition with our neighbor, or brother and sister. 'Dog eat dog' and 'Every man for themselves' are lies fed to the masses, because there's strength in numbers, and those against our success would like us to remain divided.

The rich and powerful don't adhere to those dividing clichés. They take care of their own and each other. Do you think this mindset was shared so we would all look at each other as competition and forget how strong we are as a group?

Companies run by generations of heirs, yet the rest of us are taught, it isn't necessary to help our brother. We've been taught, when hardship befalls someone we know, they not only probably deserve it, but acknowledging their situation might prompt them to ask for help!

Why does management, making twice to three times more than workers, expect workers to care equally? Why doesn't three times the reward equal three times the commitment? And one third the financial reward constitute one third the commitment? Don't we only work for the financial reward? And now people are expected to commit completely, but not receive enough compensation to offer them the simplest dreams?

**To Educators**

Everyone is teaching facts, but few are teaching how to learn. Why are private organizations offering students the ability to get better grades? You can teach students how to learn while teaching the facts associated with your subject. Though teaching how to learn is a little trickier, it will help students become everything you desire.

You've learned enough to know how to find learning techniques you can teach. Are you interested in teaching our children how to learn, or are you only concerned with teaching facts most children will find useless?

Everything that can be counted does not necessarily count; everything that counts cannot necessarily be counted.
- Albert Einstein

**To Government Leaders**

There seems to be a misunderstanding regarding who is/owns any Nation-State (country) and who is a hired manager of that Nation-State, and a misunderstanding regarding the elected leaders' place in any democratic or quasi-democratic governing systems, and I'm honored to have this opportunity to restate the basic and obvious.

The government is not the nation state (country). The citizens are the nation state (country). The elected members of government are the hired managers. Nation states give their hired managers great perks and authority. Such perks and authority, these managers lose their perspective on their position as citizens, but they're nothing more than – 1 citizen-share-owners of their country.

The President is the highest manager, with great authority, but only 1 citizen-share-owner. The Vice President is the next highest manager, but only 1 citizen-share-owner. Every manager is 1 citizen-share-owner, just like the newborns in every hospital in that nation-state.

Every citizen of every country is – 1 citizen-share-owner – often with (when they reach society approved age) – 1 citizen-share vote with regard to hiring managers, under the terms the citizens have authorized.

These hired managers are entrusted with the well-being of the society.

And some managers are trying to deny certain citizens-owners, things as basic as their 1 vote. Some managers have manipulated the well-meaning system enough to undermine the system's fail-safes, until they're no longer operable. Some managers have manipulated the society geographically to minimize the one-citizen-owner vote of some, while exaggerating the one-citizen-owner vote of others. Some have passed laws preventing certain minorities from executing their rites as citizens.

If you owned a business and your hired managers began surreptitiously undermining your ownership ...secretly doing things against your best interests... would you fire them? Government elected are hired (elected) with one, often unstated yet very real and ongoing understanding: They are to manage in the best interest of their fellow citizens, who own their nation-state and hired them.

The elected deciding they are sole owners of the Nation-State, and undermining the people who elected them, conflicts with their social duty. God manages all that is His. As Her children, some are given more responsibility than others, while given more perks than the rest. Some managers fail this primary responsibility, and should re-evaluate their perspectives. Managers are not the Nation-State. Citizens are. Please manage as if you understand this basic premise.

Please legislate equality for all. Please honor: 'With liberty and justice for all'. We all recite it. Why do we fail to honor its premise?

For those who are trying to make permanent, something the spiritual universe desires, remain temporary… To those looking to conquer physical death: You will …and it will be your greatest nightmare. It will be the greatest nightmare humans will ever experience. Not a communal human nightmare until the only humans left choose this path, but a personal specific nightmare as each individual becomes aware of what they've chosen.

You're already immortal. If this wasn't true, you wouldn't be able to create immortality. If immortality didn't already exist, it wouldn't be possible. Humans flirting with immortality prove God's immortality is feasible.

Your cost, thinking this physical life and limited resources, are where and how you wish to limit your immortality will be your greatest mistake. An unending and horrendous immortal mistake.

You will know a fright beyond your wildest imagination. A fright you cannot escape. For once chosen, there is no unchoosing. You've been warned. Will my warning stop you? You and I both know the answer.

Do we both know the actual results? I know I won't convince you of that answer, and I know why. The choice is yours. You have free will, but for your act, will not be fully aware of one aspect of your choice, until you have chosen. Please reconsider. You are already immortal.

# Chapter Fourteen
## Change

Changing paradigms

There is no *wrath of God*; only oppression and wrath from childish brothers and sisters. If God had wrath and wanted to show it against those who oppose Him and what He stands for, lessons would diminish, and the lessons are invaluable toward our immortal growth.

A continual loop story:

Saint Thomas More wrote *Utopia* in (year) 1516*

Excerpt:

"...what justice is there in this: that a nobleman, a goldsmith, a banker, or any other man, that either does nothing at all, or at best, is employed in things that are of no use to the public, should live in great luxury and splendor upon what is so ill acquired, and a mean man, a carter, a smith, or a ploughman, that works harder even than the beasts themselves, and is employed in labors so necessary, that no commonwealth could hold out a year without them, can only earn so poor a livelihood and must lead so miserable a life, that the condition of the beasts is much better than theirs?"

* Written in 1516. Five Hundred years ago. It sounds like today. Why? Have we really learned so little?

My favorite book: *War Against the Weak* by Edwin Black

You'll read it with a dropped jaw. There is a history, few of us are taught.

Proof: Most European Americans cannot answer: Where, with regard to where they're standing, did the closest post-Renaissance human genocide occur? Answer: Right where they stand.

If more of us learned the hidden events our nation is too embarrassed to share, maybe we'd be less inclined to repeat similar embarrassments.

Another brilliant learning experience: Jane Elliott – Blue Eyes. Please consider investigating this brilliant person, her findings, and her teaching.

**The Future**

Spiritual entities have the ability to communicate, and the following has been shared.

There are over 220,000 planets with intelligent life in this universe, some with interstellar travel abilities. There are roughly four million planets with life. We are aware we've been and are being visited by interstellar beings. They're monitoring our growth, and when possible, stopping our self-annihilation foolishness, but they can only do so much.

The argument for other life in the universe: Do you believe God created galaxies too numerous to count ...for no other reason than it gives our planet a pretty nighttime sky?

Interstellar travel: Travel with weapons – meet travelers with bigger weapons. Travel unarmed – travel is safe. The travelers visiting here are friendly and unarmed or they would have laid waste to humans eons ago. But we continue firing at them. The space shuttle astronaut's home movie of the two entities being identified and fired at, is proof beyond doubt humans are aware.

Their exit right before interception means: They have awareness of our hostility, our weapon capabilities, and our inability to actually harm them. They know we're here and at what level of cosmic maturity we are. They also know we're far from mature enough to enjoy their knowledge and abilities.

Concepts of spiritual existence and inter-planetary sentient entities are not interchangeable, mutually inclusive, or exclusive. All they signify is: There are wondrous new awarenesses and experiences on the other side of our voluntary childishness.

Unified theory will not be solved for centuries. A possible difficulty: We aren't counting the way this universe naturally counts. Signs accordingly are everywhere.

**Conclusion**

Do we have to abandon our current beliefs in order to move forward as a species? I don't believe so, but we would benefit from revisiting and rethinking many of the ideas we believe unquestioningly. Buddha and the Christ taught love and acceptance, and *love* and *accept* not only cost nothing, but also pay back exponentially.

Our problems don't stem from groups not adhering to antiquated childish laws, but from our nonadherence to the love, forgiveness, and acceptance philosophies our great thinkers have taught. To believe someone is a higher life-form, then not read or accept their messages is confusing. Believing in something means adhering to it, and in order to imitate a belief, it must be studied.

We're not only demonstrating a refusal to embrace our growing knowledge, but a demand we revert back to times of ignorance. We once believed the earth was thousands of years old because we didn't have the means to discover otherwise. Continuing to believe things now proven false, is more harmful than we understand. We're preventing our own progress.

Change is uncomfortable, but ongoing. Look at the Catholic organization's history for examples of an all-powerful regime trying to stop human progress…and humans still moved forward. Would you rather still believe the earth is flat and the center of the universe? Would you rather still believe angels raise and lower the Sun, or do you prefer our current knowledge?

We're moving forward. We hope you'll come along for the ride. No, we're not asking you to drive. Just stare out the window and enjoy the view.

The church says the earth is flat, but I have seen its shadow on the moon, and I have more confidence even in a shadow than in the church. – Ferdinand Magellan

Adjusting our current religious beliefs, will allow us to accept a next level of understanding – including a spiritual awareness leading to a different level of respect for spiritual and physical existence. The new millennium will be a change of culture – including how we interact with each other and our planet – but change is gradual. There will be no lifespan-altering changes …stupidity notwithstanding.

…Melted their weapons and turned them into plowshares… Those who are intelligent and courageous will like the idea. With the changes, come some fascinating perks, not yet shared. They're close enough to ask for, but we currently decline.

Humans control the events leading to the change, under the premise, the change will occur. If we don't self-annihilate, we can begin implementing the transition whenever we decide. Religious could lead the way, but seem more reluctant to conform to God's edicts, than any other group.

God isn't the manipulative repressive ogre our ancient book describes. The earth has seen many tyrants, but God isn't one. The bible or its interpretation, repositions many of God's intentions. God didn't say fear Him. Man wrote that. God didn't give us restrictions. Man did that. God said He freed us from religious law, yet many hold religious law against anyone listening.

God wants us to move forward, in wisdom, intelligence, and awareness, and man is constantly trying to block that path …mostly in God's name. Leaders especially block progress. It's the laziest way to govern. It reins in freedom, from a consciousness perspective.

Convince a group they need to be self-restrictive and the rulers win. Yet the rulers are never self-restricted. Most rulers truly believe they're above the law ruling common man. Most rulers make that statement law whenever possible.

We should instead consider giving more credence to the practical self-rule perspective: Give someone something to lose, and they won't risk losing it. And the average person asks for very little.

Leaders won't hear this message and change. They'll either ignore the message or be offended by it. It's going to be interesting seeing how many attack the author, but never refute the message, like they've done for every messenger who has ever shared this message, like Christ was abused for his efforts.

God doesn't seem to interact with the successful, as much as we tend to believe. I imagine because He'd like the love/forgive message to stand on its own. It seems God measures love and hate, internally.

Remember the default position for all things: God is Perfect. If something seems against good judgment …just not perfect – then it's a human concept or flaw incorporated into that singular primary edict: God is perfect.

Humans are imperfect. Even our understanding of *perfect* is imperfect.

Hell: The all-encompassing final and finite control of the majority of the masses. (and nothing more)

Our ruling one percent understood long ago, and understand now, they rule under one primary adage: The masses allow them. Many aren't aware of this maxim or that rulers are aware, but there isn't a ruler with any maturity, who isn't fully cognizant of this primary concept.

Populations decide who rules, whether the ruler is elected or not. Further dynamics are for a different discussion, but I mention this to explain the necessity to perpetuate the concept of a hell, as the all-inclusive conformity demand. It is nothing more than the one final largescale punishment threat for misbehavior.

One percent will fail to conform. Another few percent will walk the edge of conformity, and Hell once helped control a majority of the remaining percent. It's just one of the many controls, like religion, media, peer pressure, but it is one of the strongest concepts a ruler can use to promote conformity. History has also proven a need for the concept of a catch-all controlling agent, but a majority of current humans have demonstrated, the need for this schema is diminishing.

We're immortal beings and heaven is spiritual existence. And since God is spirit, spiritual beings can feel God's presence far easier and in far more depth, than can beings removed from God and spiritual existence due to the physical restrictions / limitations / boundaries of the physical universes.

This removal from spiritual existence isn't a test. This is an experience. We are here to experience one more page in the never-ending book of existence.

There is no eternal penalty for getting something wrong. There are only the learning experiences, getting things wrong offers, and this too is necessary to become the eventual spiritual beings we strive toward.

We will experience many existences, and all things positive and negative. Our perfect Parent is teaching His children. And you can be sure of nothing like you can be sure: you're God's eternal child. So was your father's father's father and so is your daughter and her daughter's daughter's daughter.

*Perfect*: I've had the meaning infused into my immortal being, so please forgive me for being absolute in my opinion.

Are there penalties for not abiding by God's requests? For most, there are no individual penalties. Even most preachers, preaching hate and inequality won't receive discipline in this life, nor will leaders who abuse their citizens. There are reasons and most are based on the idea, experiential learning is the best teacher, and individual lessons are rarely in the form of direct admonishment.

Some humans will notice some discipline. You know the degree with which you're disciplined. Group stupidity however, seems to produce a more direct result.

Humans insist we're the only existing intelligent life, then continually fight like hummingbirds at a never emptying hummingbird feeder. Yes, hummingbirds are sure the universe isn't big enough for two to drink from a single backyard feeder, but why are humans sure we can't coexist?

We've been fighting our neighbors since we discovered them, continually over our entire existence. And it produces nothing but population culling. When do we notice …or have we?

**Our Free Will**

Prophesies are *not* written in stone. Just the opposite. They're the spiritual world prompting us out of love, if we stay on our current course we will see corresponding results. Some groups try to adhere to these warnings like they're strict guidelines, when all we have to do is adjust away from their warning, to set a new course.

Salvation and downfall look identical. Evaluate carefully. Measure *love vs hate*.

Those who assess incorrectly will find the opposite of what they seek.

Some mistakenly think 'adhering to religious law' will prompt God to spare us from the fate our loveless choices mandate. We don't understand, we direct our fate. God does not. She hopes instead, we learn love and forgiveness …coexistence …tolerance and acceptance. Then and only then will WE have adjusted our fate.

~~~

The incidents which have led to my beliefs are complex, protracted, and disjointed, but I wish to explain specific events in further detail. This could have been added to the beginning of the book, but is best added here:

I asked God not to hide from me, a long time ago. I told Her, 'I know you exist', then begged Him, please don't hide from me.

This request may have been naïve. Like all things, it comes with parts I didn't know, when I made the request. God is overwhelming, as Aeschylus wrote. Everything about God is immeasurably, astronomically greater than humans.

I'm aware of how unusual my personal exposure to another plane of existence is. Do I know whether I have the right or duty to share my experiences? I believe this book has been requested by the spirit world. Twice I was shown the cover and title. I was also requested to write, when I decided this project was beyond my ability.

But this information is not shared for me. I already know the information and gain nothing spiritually or intellectually by sharing. I share it for your gain, that you might know, if you have similar cosmic concerns, your existence is for a wonderfully positive and meaningful reason and not the doom, disaster, or fleeting insignificance our rather antiquated and myopic ancestors claim. (See: Perfect)

I've met only three others who've experienced contact with the spirit world. One whispered a prophesy about me, to me, when I was young. We were in a group, but no one acknowledged the short sentence. The incident is vivid in my mind, and the statement has come true.

Another talked about writing a similar book and told me they've met others saying the same. It seems, the desire to share our spiritual awareness is consistent for those with comparable experiences. But knowing spiritual information, and writing these experiences makes most uncomfortable, for reasons ranging from completely personal, to broadly universal, such as *Who am I to share concepts concerning existences so fleetingly and strangely exposed?*

There are signs, others have been shown what I've been shown, and I've surmised, spiritual existence doesn't hide from everyone. I've also come to understand, after getting to know the few who are also experiencing my fate, the spiritual realm mainly interacts with a uniquely unfavored group. Some of God's children struggle with their fate in this world, and that statement summarizes some confusing occurrences.

For the few I've met, I've noticed we've all endured unusual experiences we don't share with many, but we share enough to become aware of others like us. Sometimes I'll read something and know the author is aware of more than they're sharing, as I've written hints of my experiences in different work.

My conclusion based on that information: Love versus hate is an inner revelation. No matter how it's shared, parts of the message are difficult to comprehend from an outward source. The lessons may have to be experienced before they become characteristic, which explains my experiences and subsequent perspective changes. It also confirms the reasoning behind the lessons some fringe brothers and sisters are receiving.

For those who feel confused by their place in the world or some of the world's beliefs, you're not alone in your insight, but know your experiences are making you the immortal being you'll eventually become.

This book was written solely as an attempt to expose not only more realistic spiritual models, but more accurate loving forgiving paradigms than are currently being professed. The book is shared with the hope, the new perspectives will allow you to live a less burdened life, and some enclosed concepts will help with your immortal progression.

    Please consider accepting a few simple, short lessons:
    God is perfect. (the new definition)
    Love/Forgive is the prime rule for all existence, and it transcends universes.
    Trust your perfect God. If you cannot, please understand, that is your shortcoming, not God's.
    The Golden Rule is *still* the golden rule, and it's considered the *golden* rule for a reason.
    God's last command is His most important command. (John 13:34-35) It represents the single axiom transcending all universes.

    And people gathered from far and wide just to seek the word he spread. / I'll tell you everything I've learned …and *love* was all he said. – Yusuf Islam

    So here we are. And we get to choose once again where we head from here. Well … we think we get to choose. The truth is … the intelligent don't get to choose. There are too many children voicing their opinion for anyone to listen to the few who would like to lead us in the direction we should go. And there's a spiritual reason. And no one is going to like the reason ...but here it is:

We *ALL* have to learn the lessons the wise have learned. Sharing these lessons isn't going to help anyone learn them. Only existential experience teaches the lessons. We have to experience before we learn the lessons it teaches. Like the unfortunate experience their existence, and learn.

There are two ways to learn:

1. Learn by the experience of others (the wise)
2. Learn by making the same mistakes all the humans made before us.

And you think you get to choose. But the wise way doesn't teach the lesson ...and the spirits-in-charge know it. So you too have to learn the lesson yourself. ...Whether you like it or not.

WW I was the war to end all wars ...and it didn't. The next generation never experienced it ...so they will.

WW II taught us the fallacy of race supremacy ...but it didn't. The next generation never experienced it ...so they will.

The Polish / Jew / Gypsy Holocaust was supposed to be the world's last genocide ...and there have been eight genocides since.

The continual learning loop must be exposed to everyone before anyone is allowed to move past it. The curse is: Some will get the lessons first and have to endure the wait until the rest receive the lessons.

And this is the curse some humans endure. And the children will pass the difference off, pretending those who have already learned, have no clue about what they speak. And time will always prove the accuracy of the forewarning.

There are parts to certain revelations which cannot be shared, for the same reason a math professor cannot share calculus with 4$^{th}$ graders.

This is the part of the book where I lose you. But better to lose you than pretend or lie. Many wise men have shared what direction we must head …and we refuse en-mass. Don't think our refusal is an accident, or is not recorded. Our every action is measured. And our every reaction measures us.

**Personal Conclusion**

There is advantage in the wisdom won from pain. Wisdom comes alone through suffering. – Aeschylus

For future generations, with regard to who I am, just in case things get ridiculously twisted…

I am not a god. I am a pathetic human messenger of an anonymous messenger, and wish also to remain anonymous. I'm nothing more. Certain devastating circumstances in my life have shared lessons and forced me to attempt writing. Please understand I'm human like you. And failing to understand this last point, and making me anything but your equal, disheartens me completely.

We are one human species and no one can prove otherwise.
We were all humans until race disconnected us, religion separated us, politics divided us, and wealth classified us. – Anon

I hope you'll consider questioning this document's meaning and reasoning but before you offer your assessment, can you measure your ability to evaluate the information? Do you have the ability to recognize your depth of study, and/or biased proclivities and how they might hinder your ability to appraise the proposed paradigm-shifting discomfort?

If you can honestly answer yes, please measure. And if you have a better perspective, please share. This dialog is meant to question under the premise, I question. If you have verifiable, different conclusions, I hope you'll share so I may better understand my own questions.

If you cannot measure intellectually and objectively, please choose to either study, or refrain from a dissenting opinion. You may think your personal proclivities benefit humankind, but you may be inaccurate.

If your proclivity is to attack *me* because you disagree with all or parts of my message:

If you're going to declare me garbage for my beliefs or authoring this document, you're not going to get an argument from me. I know who I am. I know my flaws and shortcomings better than anyone. I have far to go and am just trying to take my first steps toward the being I hope to someday be.

Attacking me doesn't bother me. All it means is, you're leaving someone else alone.

But when you're done attacking me, attack my words with the same ferocity. Prove the words wrong. Work until you have irrefutable proof my concepts and theories are wrong, or agree they have merit, and change misguided beliefs.

The cost if you don't? ...not my job, but you and I both know whose job it is. And at that point, hope my words are more accurate than the bullshit some others have been peddling.

# Addendum

Men occasionally stumble over the truth, but most pick themselves up and hurry off as if nothing happened. – Winston Churchill

Ignorant men raise questions, wise men answered a thousand years ago. – Johann Wolfgang von Goethe

I love trying to write quotes. Every quote in this book, with nothing more than a dash following, is mine. Here are some others. Thanks for indulging me.

Someone else's good fortune doesn't take away from mine –

Capitalism: Be careful using the bottom of the mountain to make the top higher. If you relocate too much, eventually the top will be the bottom again. –

Ignoring edicts doesn't immunize us from them –

Intelligence involves the ability to accept new information and adjust existing beliefs. –

What we don't have helps us recognize what we have, but what we have doesn't help us recognize what we don't have. –

Change your world before your world changes you. –

If you think their religion is invalid because of their hatred, why do you think yours is genuine in spite of its hatred? –

History drives literature while literature directs history. –

What if a masculine male is attracted to a masculine female who has more male characteristics and is more masculine than a feminine male? Who is what? –

Humanity moves forward, the day we realize religious books weren't written by God. –

If you identify with a political party, we're on different thinking planes. –

Our first problem with categorization is, we don't make enough categories. Our second problem is, we make too many categories. –

Ever notice how our political and religious leaders are always steps behind those changing the world? –

Never ask anyone behind you how to get further down the road you're on. –

Asking me if you could ask me a question is a question you didn't ask me if you could ask. –

Don't let the location of your seat influence your interpretation of the play. –

The less a government earns loyalty, the more it demands loyalty. –

Every religious human between you and God, doesn't belong there. –

I have no tolerance for intolerance. –

Don't look into the mirror hoping to discover who you are. Look into your heart, then tell the mirror who you are. –

Prophecies aren't written in stone. They're given so we may alter course. –

The best sentence I've ever written (in my humble opinion):

If God is love, then doesn't it only make sense that it is better to love completely wrong than it is to hate completely right? –

# Bibliography

There's no order to these, and I don't care about formatting. This isn't a college paper, and I'm not submitting it for a grade. If you've gotten this far, you've noticed the body of the document has references too. Some may repeat.

The Bible ( ☺ ) …Uncopyrighted public versions, of course. (There are humans who think they own bible copyrights – which proves humans believe the contents are of human origin.)

The Bible: So Misunderstood It's a Sin by Kurt Eichenwald

http://www.newsweek.com/2015/01/02/thats-not-what-bible-says-294018.html

http://www.huffingtonpost.com/bart-d-ehrman/the-bible-telling-lies-to_b_840301.html

http://www.nature.com/news/sex-redefined-1.16943#auth-1

http://www.auburn.edu/~allenkc/trinity.html#_1_6

http://www.theglobeandmail.com/life/science-in-transition-understanding-the-biology-behind-gender-identity/article25553156/?utm_source=facebook.com&utm_medium=Referrer%3A+Social+Network+%2F+Media&utm_campaign=Shared+Web+Article+Links&fb_ref=Default

https://www.sciencebasedmedicine.org/sex-gender-and-sexuality-its-complicated/

http://www.wouldjesusdiscriminate.org/biblical_evidence/gay_couple.html

http://www.huffingtonpost.com/john-shore/the-best-case-for-the-bible-not-condemning-homosexuality_b_1396345.html

http://www.wouldjesusdiscriminate.org/biblical_evidence/born_gay.html

http://www.religioustolerance.org/ashford00.htm#menu

http://myoutspirit.com/index.php?pag=article&id=44

http://www.christianpost.com/news/matthew-vines-says-most-christians-are-wrong-homosexuality-is-not-a-sin-82026/

http://www.wouldjesusdiscriminate.org/biblical_evidence/history_lessons.html

http://www.focusintl.com/GD060-%20Gender%20-%20biological%20theory.pdf

http://www.religioustolerance.org/ashford02.htm

http://www.who.int/genomics/gender/en/index1.html

http://listverse.com/2015/08/11/10-bible-passages-that-might-be-totally-bogus/?utm_source=more&utm_medium=link&utm_campaign=direct

http://www.isna.org/faq/what_is_intersex

https://books.google.com/books?id=evbdjAQYA1cC&pg=PA343&lpg=PA343&dq=biological+psychology+and+gender&source=bl&ots=zNWyNufVes&sig=gvbvnriZZATGbn7dZyifUkM-qc0&hl=en&sa=X&ei=Np_vUpXfDaLlyAGL4IGgCQ#v=onepage&q=biological%20psychology%20and%20gender&f=false

http://www.tertullian.org/rpearse/nicaea.html

http://www.asktheatheists.com/questions/1404-is-the-bible-plagiarized-from-other-reli/

http://web.uvic.ca/~ahdevor/HowMany/HowMany.html

http://listverse.com/2018/08/01/10-dark-and-ungodly-christian-beliefs/

http://www.huffingtonpost.com/chloe-hollett-jd/the-prevention-of-suicide-through-unconditional-love_b_8695264.html

https://www.cnn.com/2018/06/22/us/misused-bible-verses-sessions/index.html

The Definition of Normal  E S Carpenter

The Definition of Equal  E S Carpenter

The Foundation of LGBT Normality  E S Carpenter

# PostScript

You have enemies? Good. That means you've stood for something, sometime in your lifetime. - Winston Churchill

I once thought differently than I do now. I once had corporate success and believed my success was based mostly on my abilities. Then one day, while praying (Giving thanks, as the bible story suggests we should, but so seldom do) during the twenty minute walk alone from the train to my office, something whispered to me. 'You will have a downturn.'

The whisper was amazingly clear. The whisper—not the volume of a 'whisper'. The whisperer: unidentified and not of this physical realm.

The message frightened the shit out of me and made me physically and emotionally ill. The remembrance brings tears of despair to this day, thirty years later.

I'll not discuss what I believe I lost. That has no bearing on the incident, or the transformation I've gone through because of the resulting events.

I immediately asked two requests, for the necessity to taste what I was sure the words clearly stated, and both have been granted. One with a side return request from the beyond, which I have faithfully honored. The other is spiritual, and I have full trust, the Lord will not break.

I now know, we're not who we are, solely because of our abilities. There are more important things in this universe than 'being successful' teaches. Am I wise enough to know, thirty years later, the lessons would share things I had completely the wrong opinion about, and my new insight would be worth my 'downturn'? I fight to say yes, but my heart still says no. Many of the lessons were awful. What I now know, wasn't worth the pain and torture I experienced. This experience has taken more from me than I care to share, and that which doesn't kill you, may leave you far more destroyed than you can recover from. (The truthful twist to an asshole cliché.)

This experience has taught me so much, but with great almost unbearable heartache. The lessons are great…and unbelievably awful.

But being cluelessly successful wouldn't be my preferred choice either. I enjoy learning, but I also appreciate a middle-ground, and though I have no gauge what would differentiate my quantity and that quantity of lessons, I do believe my life would have been more enjoyable without the decreed downturn. I know someone who has what I exchanged, and see what lessons they've never been exposed to. Yes, I know the right answer is not my answer, but some of the lessons were awful.

But if things don't happen just like they happened, this document doesn't get written, and there seems to be a request for it, as I've mentioned before.

The title confused me when it was first shared. I thought it was terrible, until I was almost done writing and realized how many times I had used the word and how it represents the contents and my experiences. What an amazing nightmare.

Please forgive my inability to make this document everything I would hope you need. I really do think I don't have the ability to do these subjects justice. Please know that though my abilities are limited and my success nonexistent, my intention and my message are sincere. I gave my mind, heart, and soul to this endeavor, for the length of this endeavor, and truly believe all I've written.

Accept the lessons today brings. If inclined, learn them. Some are awful, but all get you closer to a magnificent Being worth any and every lesson it takes to reach.

And above all … know your perfect God loves you perfectly.

www.ingramcontent.com/pod-product-compliance
Lightning Source LLC
LaVergne TN
LVHW051037080426
835508LV00019B/1569